Poems and Readings for
Funerals and Memorials

Compiled by
Luisa Moncada

NEW
HOLLAND

Published in 2009 by New Holland Publishers (UK) Ltd
London • Cape Town • Sydney • Auckland
www.newhollandpublishers.com
Garfield House, 86–88 Edgware Road, London W2 2EA, United Kingdom
80 McKenzie Street, Cape Town 8001, South Africa
Unit 1, 66 Gibbes Street, Chatswood, NSW 2067, Australia
218 Lake Road, Northcote, Auckland, New Zealand

10 9 8 7 6 5 4 3 2

A catalogue record for this book is available from the British Library

ISBN 978 1 84773 404 4

Publishing Director: Rosemary Wilkinson
Publisher: Aruna Vasudevan
Project Editor: Julia Shone
Editorial Assistant: Cosima Hibbert
Design: Sarah Williams
DTP: Pete Gwyer
Production: Melanie Dowland

Reproduction by Pica Digital Pte. Ltd., Singapore
Printed and bound in India by Replika Press

The paper used to produce this book is sourced from sustainable forests.

for my mother and grandparents,
with much love

Contents

Foreword

This collection brings together over 100 readings from a variety of sources. Its purpose is to help people who are experiencing the despair and sorrow of a bereavement draw comfort from the words of others who have similarly experienced the death of a loved one. Many of these readings celebrate life, love and commitment and this is something that I focused on when selecting the text. This is by no means a definitive collection but I hope that you find something in the selection of traditional, contemporary, religious and non-religious poems and extracts to draw strength from.

I very much hope these readings bring you some comfort at what is an extremely difficult time and, if you have been asked to read something appropriate at a funeral or memorial service, that this collection helps to make the difficult job of choosing a suitable reading that much easier.

—Luisa Moncada

The Purpose of This Book

Organising a funeral or a memorial service for a loved one is probably one of the most stressful and upsetting things that we have to face in our life times. Although this book does not aim to give you advice on how to do this, it will hopefully help to make the choosing of a reading for the service that much easier.

Choosing your service

One of the first things you need to decide is the kind of service to have and when and where to have it. There are several options depending on how religious or non-religious the person who has died was. These include the following:

Religious funeral service – which needs to be discussed and organised with the relevant church or religious organisation.

Civil funeral service – for those people wishing to create something more personal and unique and suitable for a cremation or burial, it can be held almost anywhere you wish, other than in a religious building. Loved ones usually work with a celebrant to create the kind of ceremony they want.

Independent funeral service – for people who want to organise everything themselves and don't, for whatever reason, want to involve a funeral director. Although this may allow you to have ultimate control over the service, this is much more work than having a funeral director organise matters for you as many bereaved choose to do.

In addition, you may want to organise a **memorial service** to honour your loved one. This may involve singing or playing

favourite or meaningful songs or music, making a eulogy
and/or asking friends and relatives to read something particularly
beloved or that your loved one actually wrote.

How to Use This Book

Once you have decided on the service, apart from inviting people,
choosing flowers and so on, one of the next major tasks is
choosing your readings – but where do you start? This book aims
to help you do this.

Organised alphabetically by writer, *Poems and Readings for
Funerals and Memorials* includes traditional and contemporary,
biblical and non-religious readings from a huge range of sources,
including the Bible, books such as *The Prophet*, *The Little Prince*
and *The House at Pooh Corner*, poems by such writers as W.H.
Auden, Sylvia Plath and Alice Walker, lyrics by such song writers
as Bob Dylan and celebrated eulogies.

Each entry has a useful tag in the top left or right margin of the
page explaining what the extract is; at the bottom of the page a
short biography informs you about the author, often putting the
reading in context, just in case this is something you want to use
in the service. The book ends with an index of first lines, as quite
often people recognise the first line of a song or a poem, for
example, but do not know the actual title.

I hope this collection will help you choose a suitable reading, one
that allows you to celebrate the life of your loved one through
these often poignant and beautiful words. My thoughts and very
best wishes are with you at this time.

If I Speak in the Tongues of Men

1 CORINTHIANS 13:1—13

1 If I speak in the tongues of men and of angels, but have not love, I am only a resounding gong or clanging cymbal.

2 If I have the gift of prophecy and can fathom all mysteries, and all knowledge, and if I have a faith that can move mountains, but have not love, I am nothing.

3 If I give all I possess to the poor and surrender my body to the flames, but have not love, I gain nothing.

4 Love is patient, love is kind. It does not envy, it does not boast, it is not proud.

5 It is not rude, it is not self-seeking, it is not easily angered, it keeps no record of wrongs.

6 Love does not delight in evil but rejoices with the truth.

7 It always protects, always trusts, always hopes, always perseveres.

8 Love never fails. But where there are prophecies, they will cease; where there are tongues, they will be stilled; where there is knowledge, it will pass away.

9 For we know in part and we prophesy in part,

10 But when perfection comes, the imperfect disappears.

11 When I was a child, I talked like a child, I thought like a child, I reasoned like a child. When I became a man, I put childish ways behind me.

12 Now we see but a poor reflection as in a mirror; then we shall see face to face. Now I know in part; then I shall know fully, even as I am fully known.

13 And now these three remain: faith, hope and love. But the greatest of these is love.

15

New International Version

BIBLICAL

The Coming of the Lord

1 THESSALONIANS 4:13–18

13 Brothers, we do not want you to be ignorant about those who are asleep, or to grieve like the rest of men, who have no hope.

14 We believe that Jesus died and rose again, and so we believe that God will bring with Jesus those who have fallen asleep in him.

15 According to the Lord's own word, we tell you that we who are still alive, who are left till the coming of the Lord, will certainly not precede those who have fallen asleep.

16 For the lord himself will come down from heaven, with a loud command, with the voice of the archangel and with the trumpet call of God, and the dead in Christ will rise first.

17 After that, we who are still alive and are left will be caught up together with them in the clouds to meet the Lord in the air and so we will be with the Lord forever.

18 Therefore encourage each other with these words.

16
_____

New International Version

The God of All Comfort

BIBLICAL

2 CORINTHIANS 1:3–7

3 Praise be to the God and Father of our Lord Jesus Christ,
   the Father of compassion and the God of all comfort,
4 who comforts us in all our troubles, so that we can comfort
   those in any trouble with the comfort we ourselves have
   received from God.
5 For just as the sufferings of Christ flow over into our lives,
   so also through Christ our comfort overflows.
6 If we are distressed, it is for your comfort and salvation;
   if we are comforted, it is for your comfort, which produces
   in you patient endurance of the same sufferings we suffer.
7 And our hope for you is firm, because we know that
   just as you share in our sufferings, so also you share
   in our comfort.

17

New International Version

BIBLICAL

The Time Has Come for My Departure
2 TIMOTHY 4:6–8

6 For I am already being poured out like a drink offering,
   and the time has come for my departure.

7 I have fought the good fight, I have finished the race, I
   have kept the faith.

8 Now there is in store for me the crown of righteousness,
   which the Lord, the righteous Judge, will award to me on
   that day – and not only to me, but also to all who have
   longed for his appearing.

New International Version

18

PLAY

from Agamemnon
AESCHYLUS

Drop, drop – in our sleep, upon the heart
sorrow falls, memory's pain,
and to us, though against our very will,
even in our own despite,
comes wisdom,
by the awful grace of God.

*Aeschylus (c. 525–456 BC) is known as the father of Greek tragedy. He
wrote several epic plays.* Agamemnon, *from which this extract is taken, focuses
on the life of the King of Argos. Robert F. Kennedy used a version of this extract
in his speech following Martin Luther King, Jr.'s assassination on 4 April 1968.*

Memorial Day for the War Dead

POEM

Yehuda Amichai

Memorial day for the war dead. Add now
the grief of all your losses to their grief,
even of a woman that has left you. Mix
sorrow with sorrow, like time-saving history,
which stacks holiday and sacrifice and mourning
on one day for easy, convenient memory.

Oh, sweet world soaked, like bread,
in sweet milk for the terrible toothless God.
'Behind all this some great happiness is hiding.'
No use to weep inside and to scream outside.
Behind all this perhaps some great happiness is hiding.

19

Memorial day. Bitter salt is dressed up
as a little girl with flowers.
The streets are cordoned off with ropes,
for the marching together of the living and the dead.
Children with a grief not their own march slowly,
like stepping over broken glass.

The flautist's mouth will stay like that for many days.
A dead soldier swims above little heads
with the swimming movements of the dead,
with the ancient error the dead have
about the place of the living water.

A flag loses contact with reality and flies off.
A shopwindow is decorated with
dresses of beautiful women, in blue and white.
And everything in three languages:
Hebrew, Arabic, and Death.

A great and royal animal is dying
all through the night under the jasmine
tree with a constant stare at the world.

A man whose son died in the war walks in the street
like a woman with a dead embryo in her womb.
'Behind all this some great happiness is hiding.'

Yehudi Amichai (1924–2000) was a German-born Israeli poet. He published several volumes of poetry, two novels and a book of short stories. His work has been translated into 33 languages.

Refusal

POEM

MAYA ANGELOU

Beloved,
In what other lives or lands
Have I known your lips
Your Hands
Your Laughter brave
Irreverent.
Those sweet excesses that
I do adore.
What surety is there
That we will meet again,
On other worlds some
Future time undated.
I defy my body's haste.
Without the promise
Of one more sweet encounter
I will not deign to die

Maya Angelou (b. 1928) is an African American writer, actor and broadcaster. She was part of the Harlem Writers Guild and was involved in the American Civil Rights Movement, working closely with Malcolm X until his assassination in 1965. She has written more than 30 books.

A Thousand Winds

ANON

Do not stand at my grave and weep,
I am not there, I do not sleep.

I am in a thousand winds that blow,
I am the softly falling snow.
I am the gentle showers of rain,
I am the fields of ripening grain.

I am in the morning hush,
I am in the graceful rush
Of beautiful birds in circling flight,
I am the starshine of the night.
I am in the flowers that bloom,
I am in a quiet room.

I am in the birds that sing,
I am in each lovely thing.
Do not stand at my grave and cry,
I am not there. I did not die.

*Although this poem is mostly attributed to an anonymous source, some
believe that Mary Elizabeth Frye (1905–2004) wrote it to console a
friend whose mother was dying.*

Indian Prayer

SPIRITUAL

ANON

When I am dead
Cry for me a little
Think of me sometimes
But not too much.

Think of me now and again
As I was in life
At some moments it's pleasant to recall
But not for long.

Leave me in peace
And I shall leave you in peace
And while you live
Let your thoughts be with the living.

23

POEM

Poem

ANON

Not, how did he die, but how did he live?
Not, what did he gain, but what did he give?
These are the units to measure the worth
Of a man as a man, regardless of birth.
Not what was his church, nor what was his creed?
But had he befriended those really in need?
Was he ever ready, with word of good cheer,
To bring back a smile, to banish a tear?
Not what did the sketch in the newspaper say,
But how many were sorry when he passed away?

I Thought I'd Write My Own Obituary

POEM

SIMON ARMITAGE

I thought I'd write my own obituary. Instead,
I wrote the poem for when I'm risen from the dead:

Ignite the flares, connect the phones, wind all the clocks;
the sun goes rusty like a medal in its box –
collect it from the loft. Peg out the stars,
replace the bulbs of Jupiter and Mars.
A man like that takes something with him when he dies,
but he has wept the coins that rested on his eyes,
eased out the stopper from the mouthpiece of the cave,
exhumed his own white body from the grave.

Unlock the rivers, hoist the dawn and launch the sea.
Set up the skittles of the orchard and the wood again,
now everything is clear and straight and free and good again.

*Simon Armitage (b. 1963) is an English poet, playwright
and novelist.*

Funeral Blues [Song IX]

W.H. AUDEN

Stop all the clocks, cut off the telephone,
Prevent the dog from barking with a juicy bone,
Silence the pianos and with muffled drum
Bring out the coffin, let the mourners come.

Let aeroplanes circle moaning overhead
Scribbling on the sky the message He Is Dead,
Put crepe bows round the white necks of the public doves,
Let the traffic policemen wear black cotton gloves.

He was my North, my South, my East and West,
My working week and my Sunday rest,
My noon, my midnight, my talk, my song;
I thought that love would last for ever; I was wrong.

The stars are not wanted now: put out every one;
Pack up the moon and dismantle the sun;
Pour away the ocean and sweep up the wood,
For nothing now can ever come to any good.

W. H. Auden (1907–1973) is probably one of the best-known English poets of the 20th Century. This poem, which many people recognise from the film Four Weddings and a Funeral, *was first published as 'Song IX' but was reprinted under the present title three years after Auden's death.*

The Unknown Citizen

POEM

W.H. AUDEN

(To JS/07 M 378 This Marble Monument Is Erected by the State)

He was found by the Bureau of Statistics to be
One against whom there was no official complaint,
And all the reports on his conduct agree
That, in the modern sense of an old-fashioned word, he
 was a saint,
For in everything he did he served the Greater Community.
Except for the War till the day he retired
He worked in a factory and never got fired,
But satisfied his employers, Fudge Motors Inc.
Yet he wasn't a scab or odd in his views,
For his Union reports that he paid his dues,
(Our report on his Union shows it was sound)
And our Social Psychology workers found
That he was popular with his mates and liked a drink.
The Press are convinced that he bought a paper every day
And that his reactions to advertisements were normal in
 every way.
Policies taken out in his name prove that he was fully insured,
And his Health-card shows he was once in hospital but left
 it cured.
Both Producers Research and High-Grade Living declare
He was fully sensible to the advantages of the Instalment Plan
And had everything necessary to the Modern Man,
A phonograph, a radio, a car and a frigidaire.

Our researchers into Public Opinion are content
That he held the proper opinions for the time of year;
When there was peace, he was for peace: when there was
 war, he went
He was married and added five children to the population,
Which our Eugenist says was the right number for a parent of
 his generation.
And our teachers report that he never interfered with their
 education.
Was he free? Was he happy? The question is absurd:
Had anything been wrong, we should certainly have heard.

Sonnet 20
from Sonnets from the Portuguese

POEM

ELIZABETH BARRETT BROWNING

Beloved, my Beloved, when I think
That thou wast in the world a year ago,
What time I sat alone here in the snow
And saw no footprint, heard the silence sink
No moment at thy voice, but, link by link,
Went counting all my chains as if that so
They never could fall off at any blow
Struck by thy possible hand, – why, thus I drink
Of life's great cup of wonder! Wonderful,
Never to feel thee thrill the day or night
With personal act or speech, – nor ever cull
Some prescience of thee with the blossoms white
Thou sawest growing! Atheists are as dull,
Who cannot guess God's presence out of sight.

29

Elizabeth Barrett Browning (1806–1861) is amongst the greatest English poets. Much of her writing was inspired by her love for her husband, Robert Browning. Sonnets from the Portuguese, published in 1850, is a collection of love sonnets written during their courtship.

POEM

Sonnet 43
from Sonnets from the Portuguese
ELIZABETH BARRETT BROWNING

How do I love thee? Let me count the ways.
I love thee to the depth and breadth and height
My soul can reach, when feeling out of sight
For the ends of Being and ideal Grace.
I love thee to the level of everyday's
Most quiet need, by sun and candlelight.
I love thee freely, as men strive for Right;
I love thee purely, as they turn from Praise.
I love thee with the passion put to use
In my old griefs, and with my childhood's faith.
I love thee with a love I seemed to lose
With my lost saints, I love thee with the breath,
Smiles, tears, of all my life! and, if God choose,
I shall but love thee better after death.

from Gift of Peace

READING

CARDINAL JOSEPH BERNARDIN

As I write these final words, my heart is filled with joy. I am at peace.

It is the first day of November, and fall is giving way to winter. Soon the trees will lose the vibrant colours of their leaves and snow will cover the ground. The earth will shut down, and people will race to and from their destinations bundled up for warmth. Chicago winters are harsh. It is a time of dying.

But we know that spring will soon come with all its new life and wonder ...

Many people have asked me to tell them about heaven and the afterlife. I sometimes smile at the request because I do not know any more than they do. Yet, when one young man asked if I looked forward to being united with God and all those who have gone before me, I made a connection to something I said earlier in this book. The first time I travelled with my mother and sister to my parents' homeland of Tonadico di Primiero, in northern Italy, I felt as if I had been there before. After years of looking through my mother's photo albums, I knew the mountains, the land, the houses, the people. As soon as we entered the valley, I said, 'My God, I know this place. I am home.' Somehow I think crossing from this life into life eternal will be similar. I will be home.

Cardinal Joseph Bernardin (1928–1996) was a leading theologian, who helped shape the Catholic Church in the United States.

READING

from Letters and Papers from Prison

DIETRICH BONHOEFFER

Nothing can make up for the absence of someone
whom we love, and it would be wrong to try to
find a substitute; we must simply hold out and
see it through. That sounds very hard at first,
but at the same time it is a great consolation,
for the gap, as long as it remains unfilled,
preserves the bonds between us. It is nonsense
to say that God fills the gap; God doesn't fill it,
but on the contrary, keeps it empty and so
helps us to keep alive our former communion
with each other, even at the cost of pain.

32

_Dietrich Bonhoeffer (1906–1945) was a theologian and spiritual
advisor, prominent in the Protestant Church's fight against the Nazi government..
He was sent to Flossenbürg concentration camp in Bavaria, Germany, and
executed on 9 April 1945 for his role in the resistance._

from The Order for the Burial of the Dead

BOOK OF COMMON PRAYER

Thou knowest, LORD, the secrets of our hearts;
shut not thy merciful ears to our prayer; but spare
us, LORD most holy, O GOD most mighty, O holy
and merciful SAVIOUR; thou most worthy Judge
eternal, suffer us not, at our last hour, for any pains
of death, to fall from thee.

*The Book of Common Prayer is a liturgical book used by Anglican
churches. First authorised by the Church of England in 1549, the revised
version of 1667 has continued as the standard within most Anglican
churches of the British Commonwealth.*

My Death

JACQUES BREL

My death is like
a swinging door
a patient girl who knows the score
whistle for her
and the passing time

My death waits like
a bible truth
at the funeral of my youth
weep loud for that
and the passing time

My death waits like
a witch at night
and surely as our love is bright
let's laugh for us
and the passing time

But whatever is behind the door
there is nothing much to do
angel or devil I don't care
for in front of that door
there is you

My death waits like
a beggar blind
who sees the world with an unlit mind
throw him a dime
for the passing time

My death waits
to allow my friends
a few good times before it ends
let's drink to that
and the passing time

My death waits in
your arms, your thighs
your cool fingers will close my eyes
let's not talk about
the passing time

But whatever is behind the door
there is nothing much to do
angel or devil I don't care
for in front of that door
there is you

My death waits
among the falling leaves
in magicians, mysterious sleeves
rabbits, dogs
and the passing times

My death waits
among the flowers
where the blackish shadow cowers
let's pick lilacs
for the passing time

My death waits in
a double bed
sails of oblivion at my head
pull up the sheets
against the passing time

But whatever is behind the door
there is nothing much to do
angel or devil I don't care
for in front of that door
there is you.

Jaques Brel (1929–1978) was a renowned Belgian singer-songwriter. This song, whose words were translated into English by Mort Shuman and Eric Blau, has been recorded by many musicians, including Scott Walker.

A Reminiscence

POEM

ANNE BRONTË

Yes, thou art gone! and never more
Thy sunny smile shall gladden me;
But I may pass the old church door,
And pace the floor that covers thee,

May stand upon the cold, damp stone,
And think that, frozen, lies below
The lightest heart that I have known,
The kindest I shall ever know.

Yet, though I cannot see thee more,
'Tis still a comfort to have seen;
And though thy transient life is o'er,
'Tis sweet to think that thou hast been;

To think a soul so near divine,
Within a form so angel fair,
United to a heart like thine,
Has gladdened once our humble sphere.

*Anne Brontë (1820–1849) was an English poet and novelist.
Originally entitled 'Yes Thou Art Gone', this poem was retitled, 'A
Reminiscence' when published in* Poems by Currer, Ellis and Acton
Bell, *the pseudomyms of Charlotte, Emily and Anne Brontë.*

Farewell

ANNE BRONTË

Farewell to thee! But not farewell
To all my fondest thoughts of thee;
Within my heart they still shall dwell
And they shall cheer and comfort me.

O beautiful, and full of grace!
If thou hadst never met mine eye,
I had not dreamed a living face
Could fancied charms so far outvie.

If I may ne'er behold again
That form and face so dear to me,
Nor hear thy voice, still would I fain
Preserve for aye their memory.

That voice, the magic of whose tone
Can wake an echo in my breast,
Creating feelings that, alone,
Can make my trancèd spirit blest.

That laughing eye, whose sunny beam
My memory would not cherish less;
And oh, that smile! whose joyous gleam
No mortal language can express.

On the Death of Anne Brontë

POEM

CHARLOTTE BRONTË

There's little joy in life for me,
And little terror in the grave;
I've lived the parting hour to see
Of one I would have died to save.

Calmly to watch the failing breath,
Wishing each sigh might be the last;
Longing to see the shade of death
O'er those belovèd features cast.

The cloud, the stillness that must part
The darling of my life from me;
And then to thank God from my heart,
To thank Him well and fervently;

Although I knew that we had lost
The hope and glory of our life;
And now, benighted, tempest-tossed,
Must bear alone the weary strife.

*Charlotte Brontë (1816–1855), English writer and eldest of the Brontë
sisters, is probably most famous for writing* Jane Eyre *and* Villette.
*She saw both her brother Branwell and sister Emily die in 1848. When her sister
Anne died in 1849, Charlotte wrote this poem to her, telling of her extreme grief.*

Death

EMILY BRONTË

Death! that struck when I was most confiding.
In my certain faith of joy to be –
Strike again, Time's withered branch dividing
From the fresh root of Eternity!

Leaves, upon Time's branch, were growing brightly,
Full of sap, and full of silver dew;
Birds beneath its shelter gathered nightly;
Daily round its flowers the wild bees flew.

Sorrow passed, and plucked the golden blossom;
Guilt stripped off the foliage in its pride
But, within its parent's kindly bosom,
Flowed for ever Life's restoring tide.

Little mourned I for the parted gladness,
For the vacant nest and silent song –
Hope was there, and laughed me out of sadness;
Whispering, 'Winter will not linger long!'

And, behold! with tenfold increase blessing,
Spring adorned the beauty-burdened spray;
Wind and rain and fervent heat, caressing,
Lavished glory on that second May!

High it rose – no winged grief could sweep it;
Sin was scared to distance with its shine;
Love, and its own life, had power to keep it
From all wrong – from every blight but thine!

Cruel Death! The young leaves droop and languish;
Evening's gentle air may still restore –
No! the morning sunshine mocks my anguish –
Time, for me, must never blossom more!

Strike it down, that other boughs may flourish
Where that perished sapling used to be;
Thus, at least, its mouldering corpse will nourish
That from which it sprung – Eternity.

Emily Brontë (1818–1848) was one of the famous Brontë sisters, who wrote poems and novels. Emily is probably best known for her novel Wuthering Heights. *This poem was written on 10 April 1845.*

POEM

The Soldier

RUPERT BROOKE

If I should die, think only this of me:
That there's some corner of a foreign field
That is for ever England. There shall be
In that rich earth a richer dust concealed;
A dust whom England bore, shaped, made aware,
Gave, once, her flowers to love, her ways to roam,
A body of England's, breathing English air,
Washed by the rivers, blest by suns of home.

And think, this heart, all evil shed away,
A pulse in the eternal mind, no less
Gives somewhere back the thoughts by England given;
Her sights and sounds; dreams happy as her day;
And laughter, learnt of friends; and gentleness,
In hearts at peace, under an English heaven.

Rupert Brooke (1885–1915) was an English war poet.
Originally entitled 'The Recruit', this sonnet, written in 1914,
was part of five sonnets entitled The War Sonnets.

from The Pilgrim's Progress

NOVEL

JOHN BUNYAN

I see myself now at the end of my journey; my toilsome days are ended. I am going now to see that head which was crowned with thorns, and that face which was spit upon for me. I have formerly lived by hearsay and faith, but now I go where I shall live by sight, and shall be with Him in whose company I delight myself. I have loved to hear my Lord spoken of; and wherever I have seen the print of his shoe in the earth, there I have coveted to set my foot too. His name to me has been as a civet-box; yea, sweeter than all perfumes. His voice to me has been most sweet; and his countenance I have more desired than they that have most desired the light of the sun. His word I did use to gather for my food, and for antidotes against my faintings. He has held me, and has kept me from mine iniquities; yea, my steps hath he strengthened in his way.

43

Now, while he was thus in discourse, his countenance changed; his strong man bowed under him; and after he had said, 'Take me, for I come unto Thee!' he ceased to be seen of them.

But glorious it was to see how the open region was filled with horses and chariots, with trumpeters and pipers, with singers and players on stringed instruments, to welcome the pilgrims as they went up, and followed one another in at the beautiful gate of the city.

John Bunyan (1628–1688) was an English preacher. Imprisoned on many occasions for unlicensed preaching, he wrote The Pilgrim's Progress *while incarcerated in prison in Bedford, England. The book immediately brought him great success.*

When We Two Parted

LORD BYRON

When we two parted
  In silence and tears,
Half broken-hearted
  To sever for years,
Pale grew thy cheek and cold,
  Colder thy kiss;
Truly that hour foretold
  Sorrow to this.

The dew of the morning
  Sunk chill on my brow –
It felt like the warning
  Of what I feel now.
Thy vows are all broken,
  And light is thy fame;
I hear thy name spoken,
  And share in its shame.

They name thee before me,
  A knell to mine ear;
A shudder comes o'er me –
  Why wert thou so dear?

They know not I knew thee,
  Who knew thee too well –
Long, long shall I rue thee,
  Too deeply to tell.

In secret we met –
  In silence I grieve,
That thy heart could forget,
  Thy spirit deceive.
If I should meet thee
  After long years,
How should I greet thee? –
  With silence and tears.

*Lord George Gordon Noel Byron (1788–1824) was a
London-born poet and famous figure of society. He characterised the
'Byronic hero', a defiant, melancholy young man, brooding on some
mysterious, unforgivable event in his past.*

POEM

Gravy

RAYMOND CARVER

No other word will do. For that's what it was.
Gravy.
Gravy, these past ten years.
Alive, sober, working, loving, and
being loved by a good woman. Eleven years
ago he was told he had six months to live
at the rate he was going. And he was going
nowhere but down. So he changed his ways
somehow. He quit drinking! And the rest?
After that it was all gravy, every minute
of it, up to and including when he was told about,
well, some things that were breaking down and
building up inside his head. 'Don't weep for me,'
he said to his friends. 'I'm a lucky man.
I've had ten years longer than I or anyone
expected. Pure Gravy. And don't forget it.'

46
_____

Raymond Carver (1939–1988) was an American poet and short-story writer who has influenced generations of writers. He was married to the poet Tess Gallagher, whose work also features in this book (see pages 66–68).

I'm Here for a Short Visit Only

NOEL COWARD

POEM

I'm here for a short visit only,
And I'd rather be loved than hated.
Eternity may be lonely
When my body's disintegrated;
And that which is loosely termed my soul
Goes whizzing off through the infinite
By means of some vague remote control.
I'd like to think I was missed a bit.

47

Noel Coward (1899–1973) was an acclaimed English author, dramatist, wit and actor. He also produced several films based on his own scripts, including Brief Encounter *(1945).*

dying is fine)but Death*

E.E. CUMMINGS

dying is fine)but Death

?o
baby
i

wouldn't like

Death if Death
were
good:for

48

when(instead of stopping to think)you

begin to feel of it,dying
's miraculous
why?be

cause dying is

perfectly natural;perfectly
putting
it mildly lively(but

Death

is strictly
scientific
& artificial &

evil & legal)

we thank thee
god
almighty for dying
(forgive us,o life!the sin of Death

*The punctuation and spacing used represents the author's
original manuscript.

*E.E. Cummings (1894–1962) was an American poet known for his
experimental style. He visually shaped poems, using a unique and personal
grammar and breaking up and putting together words. He often tied this to
a traditional and romantic subject matter.*

POEM

Because I Could Not Stop for Death

EMILY DICKINSON

Because I could not stop for Death –
He kindly stopped for me –
The Carriage held but just Ourselves –
And Immortality.

We slowly drove – He knew no haste
And I had put away
My labour and my leisure too,
For His Civility –

We passed the School, where Children strove
At Recess – in the Ring –
We passed the Fields of Gazing Grain –
We passed the Setting Sun –

Or rather – He passed Us –
The Dews drew quivering and chill –
For only Gossamer, my Gown –
My Tippet – only Tulle –

We paused before a House that seemed
A Swelling of the Ground –
The Roof was scarcely visible –
The Cornice – in the Ground –

Since then – 'tis Centuries – and yet
Feels shorter than the Day
I first surmised the Horses' Heads
Were toward Eternity

51

Emily Dickinson (1830–1886) is considered the most original of 19th-century American poets, noted for her unconventional broken rhyming metre and use of dashes and random capitalisation. Most of Dickinson's work remained unknown until after her death.

POEM

I Measure Every Grief I Meet

EMILY DICKINSON

I measure every Grief I meet
With narrow, probing, Eyes –
I wonder if It weighs like Mine –
Or has an Easier size.

I wonder if They bore it long –
Or did it just begin –
I could not tell the Date of Mine –
It feels so old a pain –

I wonder if it hurts to live –
And if They have to try –
And whether – could They choose between –
It would not be – to die –

I note that Some – gone patient long –
At length, renew their smile –
An imitation of a Light
That has so little Oil –

I wonder if when Years have piled –
Some Thousands – on the Harm –
That hurt them early – such a lapse
Could give them any Balm –

Or would they go on aching still
Through Centuries of Nerve –
Enlightened to a larger Pain –
In Contrast with the Love –

The Grieved – are many – I am told –
There is the various Cause –
Death – is but one – and comes but once –
And only nails the eyes –

There's Grief of Want – and grief of Cold –
A sort they call 'Despair' –
There's Banishment from native Eyes –
In Sight of Native Air –

And though I may not guess the kind –
Correctly – yet to me
A piercing Comfort it affords
In passing Calvary –

To note the fashions – of the Cross –
And how they're mostly worn –
Still fascinated to presume
That Some – are like My Own –

POEM

Not In Vain

EMILY DICKINSON

If I can stop one heart from breaking,
I shall not live in vain:
If I can ease one life the aching,
Or cool one pain,
Or help one fainting robin
Unto his nest again,
I shall not live in vain.

Tie the Strings to My Life, My Lord

EMILY DICKINSON

POEM

Tie the Strings to my Life, My Lord,
Then I am ready to go!
Just a look at the Horses –
Rapid! That will do!

Put me in on the firmest side,
So I shall never fall;
For we must ride to the Judgment,
And it's partly down Hill.

But never I mind the bridges,
And never I mind the Sea;
Held fast in Everlasting Race
By my own Choice and Thee.

Goodbye to the Life I used to live,
And the World I used to know;
And kiss the Hills for me, just once;
Now I am ready to go!

55

POEM

Sonnet 10
from the Holy Sonnets
JOHN DONNE

Death be not proud, though some have called thee
Mighty and dreadfull, for, thou art not soe,
For, those, whom thou think'st, thou dost overthrow,
Die not, poore death, nor yet canst thou kill mee.
From rest and sleepe, which but thy pictures bee,
Much pleasure, then from thee, much more must flow,
And soonest our best men with thee doe goe,
Rest of their bones, and soules deliverie.
Thou art slave to Fate, Chance, kings, and desperate men,
And dost with poyson, warre, and sicknesse dwell,
And poppie, or charmes can make us sleepe as well,
And better than thy stroake; why swell'st thou then?
One short sleepe past, wee wake eternally,
And death shall be no more; death, thou shalt die.

READING

Meditation 17
JOHN DONNE

... No man is an island, entire of itself; every man is a piece
of the continent, a part of the main. If a clod be washed away
by the sea, Europe is the less, as well as if a promontory were,
as well as if a manor of thy friend's or of thine own were. Any
man's death diminishes me, because I am involved in mankind;
and therefore never send to know for whom the bell tolls; it
tolls for thee ...

*John Donne (1573–1621) was a Protestant reformer in the court of
English King James I (James VI of Scotland). Although more often known as a
poem, these words were written by John Donne as prose. The passage is taken
from the 1624 Meditation 17, from* Devotions Upon Emergent Occasions.

A Valediction:
Forbidding Mourning

POEM

JOHN DONNE

As virtuous men pass mildly away,
And whisper to their souls to go,
Whilst some of their sad friends do say,
'The breath goes now,' and some say, 'No,'

So let us melt, and make no noise,
No tear-floods, nor sigh-tempests move;
'Twere profanation of our joys
To tell the laity our love.

Moving of the earth brings harms and fears,
Men reckon what it did and meant;
But trepidation of the spheres,
Though greater far, is innocent.

Dull sublunary lovers' love
(Whose soul is sense) cannot admit
Absence, because it doth remove
Those things which elemented it.

But we, by a love so much refined
That our selves know not what it is,
Inter-assured of the mind,
Care less, eyes, lips, and hands to miss.

Our two souls therefore, which are one,
Though I must go, endure not yet
A breach, but an expansion.
Like gold to airy thinness beat.

If they be two, they are two so
As stiff twin compasses are two:
Thy soul, the fixed foot, makes no show
To move, but doth, if the other do;

And though it in the centre sit,
Yet when the other far doth roam,
It leans, and hearkens after it,
And grows erect, as that comes home.

Such wilt thou be to me, who must,
Like the other foot, obliquely run;
Thy firmness makes my circle just,
And makes me end where I begun.

Death Is Not the End

BOB DYLAN

When you're sad and when you're lonely
And you haven't got a friend
Just remember that death is not the end

And all that you held sacred
Falls down and does not mend
Just remember that death is not the end
Not the end, not the end
Just remember that death is not the end

When you're standing on the crossroads
That you cannot comprehend
Just remember that death is not the end

And all your dreams have vanished
And you don't know what's up the bend
Just remember that death is not the end
Not the end, not the end
Just remember that death is not the end

When the storm clouds gather round you
And heavy rains descend
Just remember that death is not the end

59

And there's no-one there to comfort you
With a helping hand to lend
Just remember that death is not the end
Not the end, not the end
Just remember that death is not the end

For the tree of life is growing
Where the spirit never dies
And the bright light of salvation
Up in dark and empty skies
When the cities are on fire
With the burning flesh of men
Just remember that death is not the end

When you search in vain to find
Some law-abiding citizen
Just remember that death is not the end

Not the end, not the end
Just remember that death is not the end
Not the end, not the end
Just remember that death is not the end

Bob Dylan (b. 1941) is one of the pioneering musicians of the 20th century. His music is often concerned with political and social themes and his style has ranged from revivalist folk music to rock. This song is from his 1988 album Down in the Groove *and has been covered by many artists, including Nick Cave.*

All Return Again

RALPH WALDO EMERSON

It is the secret of the world that all things subsist
and do not die, but only retire a little from sight and
afterwards return again. Nothing is dead; men feign
themselves dead, and endure mock funerals and
mournful obituaries, and there they stand looking
out of the window, sound and well, in some new
strange disguise. Jesus is not dead; he is very well
alive; nor John, nor Paul, nor Mahomet, nor Aristotle;
at times we believe we have seen them all, and could
easily tell the names under which they go.

61

*Ralph Waldo Emerson (1803–1882) was an American
essayist and poet.*

POEM

Death Is a Fisherman

BENJAMIN FRANKLIN

Death is a fisherman, the world we see
His fish-pond is, and we the fishes be;
His net some general sickness; howe'er he
Is not so kind as other fishers be;
For if they take one of the smaller fry,
They throw him in again, he shall not die:
But death is sure to kill all he can get,
And all is fish with him that comes to net.

Benjamin Franklin (1706–1790) is best known as one of America's Founding Fathers. He helped draft the Declaration of Independence and was a leading abolitionist. He was also a printer, publisher, poet and inventor.

Nothing Gold Can Stay

ROBERT FROST

POEM

Nature's first green is gold,
Her hardest hue to hold
Her early leaf's a flower;
But only so an hour.
Then leaf subsides to leaf.
So Eden sank to grief,
So dawn goes down to day.
Nothing gold can stay.

Out, Out

ROBERT FROST

POEM

The buzz-saw snarled and rattled in the yard
And made dust and dropped stove-length sticks of wood,
Sweet-scented stuff when the breeze drew across it.
And from there those that lifted eyes could count
Five mountain ranges one behind the other
Under the sunset far into Vermont.
And the saw snarled and rattled, snarled and rattled,
As it ran light, or had to bear a load.

And nothing happened: day was all but done.
Call it a day, I wish they might have said
To please the boy by giving him the half hour
That a boy counts so much when saved from work.
His sister stood beside them in her apron
To tell them 'Supper.' At the word, the saw,
As if to prove saws knew what supper meant,
Leaped out at the boy's hand, or seemed to leap –
He must have given the hand. However it was,
Neither refused the meeting. But the hand!
The boy's first outcry was a rueful laugh,
As he swung toward them holding up the hand
Half in appeal, but half as if to keep
The life from spilling. Then the boy saw all –
Since he was old enough to know, big boy
Doing a man's work, though a child at heart –
He saw all spoiled. 'Don't let him cut my hand off –
The doctor, when he comes. Don't let him, sister!'
So. But the hand was gone already.
The doctor put him in the dark of ether.
He lay and puffed his lips out with his breath.
And then – the watcher at his pulse took fright.
No one believed. They listened at his heart.
Little – less – nothing! – and that ended it.
No more to build on there. And they, since they
Were not the one dead, turned to their affairs.

Robert Frost (1874–1963) is a central figure in the American poetic canon and this poem first appeared in Frost's 1923 volume, New Hampshire, *his first book to win a Pulitzer Prize.*

The Road Not Taken

POEM

ROBERT FROST

Two roads diverged in a yellow wood,
And sorry I could not travel both
And be one traveller, long I stood
And looked down one as far as I could
To where it bent in the undergrowth;

Then took the other, as just as fair
And having perhaps the better claim,
Because it was grassy and wanted wear;
Though as for that, the passing there
Had worn them really about the same,

And both that morning equally lay
In leaves no step had trodden black
Oh, I kept the first for another day!
Yet knowing how way leads on to way,
I doubted if I should ever come back.

I shall be telling this with a sigh
Somewhere ages and ages hence:
Two roads diverged in a wood, and I
I took the one less travelled by,
And that has made all the difference.

65

POEM

Legend with Sea Breeze

TESS GALLAGHER

When you died I wanted at least to ring
some bells, but there were only clocks
in my town and one emblematic clapper
mounted in a pseudo-park for veterans.
If there had been bells I would have
rung them, the way they used to sound
school bells in the country so children
in my mother's time seemed lit
from the other side with desire
as they ran in from the fields
with schoolbooks over their shoulders.
Once more a yellow infusion of bells

empties like a vat of canaries into
the heart so it is over-full and
the air stumbles above rooftops, and death
in its quicksilver-echo shakes
our marrow with a yellow, trilling
silence. I would have given you that,
though these nightshift workers,
these drinkers in childless taverns, these mothers
of daughters seduced at fourteen – what
can the language of bells say to them
they haven't known first as swallows
blunting the breastbone? No, better

to lead my black horse into that grove
of hemlock and stand awhile. Better
to follow it up Blue Mountain Road
and spend the day with sword ferns,
with the secret agitations of creaturely

forest-loneliness. Or to forage
like a heat-stunned bear
raking the brambles for berries and thinking
only winter, winter, and of crawling
in daylight into the beautiful excess of earth
to meet an equal excess of sleep.
Oh my black horse, what's

the hurry? Stop awhile. I want to carve
his initials into this living tree.
I'm not quite empty enough to believe he's gone,
and that's why the smell of the sea
refreshes these silent boughs, and why
some breath of him is added if I mar the ritual,
if I put utter blackness to use
so a tremor reaches him as hoofbeats, as
my climbing up onto his velvet shoulders
with only love, thunderous sea-starved love,
so in the little town where they lived

67

they won't exaggerate when they say
in their stone-coloured voices

that a horse and a woman flew down
from the mountain, and their eyes looked out
the same, like the petals of black pansies
schoolchildren press into the hollow
at the base of their throats as a sign

of their secret, wordless invincibility.
Whatever you do, don't let them ring any bells.
I'm tired of schooling, of legends, of
those ancient sacrificial bodies dragged to death
by chariots. I just want to ride my black horse,
to see where he goes.

Tess Gallagher (b. 1943) is an American poet, essayist, novelist and dramatist. She wrote this poem as part of the collection, Moon Crossing Bridge, *in memory of her late husband, the writer Raymond Carver, whose work also appears in this book (*see page 46*).*

On Joy and Sorrow,
from The Prophet

KAHLIL GIBRAN

SPIRITUAL

... Then a woman said, Speak to us of Joy and Sorrow.
And he answered:
Your joy is your sorrow unmasked.
And the selfsame well from which your laughter rises was
oftentimes filled with your tears.
And how else can it be?
The deeper that sorrow carves into your being, the more
joy you can contain.
Is not the cup that holds your wine the very cup that was
burned in the potter's oven?
And is not the lute that soothes your spirit, the very wood
that was hollowed with knives?
When you are joyous, look deep into your heart and you
shall find it is only that which has given you sorrow that is
giving you joy.
When you are sorrowful look again in your heart, and you
shall see that in truth you are weeping for that which has
been your delight.
Some of you say, 'Joy is greater than sorrow,' and others
say, 'Nay, sorrow is the greater.'
But I say unto you, they are inseparable.
Together they come, and when one sits alone with you at your
board, remember that the other is asleep upon your bed.

69

*Kahlil Gibran (1883–1931) was born in the Lebanon and is among the most
important and influential Arabic language authors of the early 20th century.* The
Prophet *(1923), which examines subjects such as life, love, children and death, is
his most celebrated statement about the truths of human experience.*

POEM

from An Elegy Written in a Country Churchyard

THOMAS GRAY

The curfew tolls the knell of parting day,
The lowing herd wind slowly o'er the lea
The plowman homeward plods his weary way,
And leaves the world to darkness and to me.

Now fades the glimm'ring landscape on the sight,
And all the air a solemn stillness holds,
Save where the beetle wheels his droning flight,
And drowsy tinklings lull the distant folds;

Save that from yonder ivy-mantled tow'r
The moping owl does to the moon complain
Of such, as wand'ring near her secret bow'r,
Molest her ancient solitary reign.

Beneath those rugged elms, that yew-tree's shade,
Where heaves the turf in many a mould'ring heap,
Each in his narrow cell for ever laid,
The rude forefathers of the hamlet sleep.

The breezy call of incense-breathing Morn,
The swallow twitt'ring from the straw-built shed,
The cock's shrill clarion, or the echoing horn,
No more shall rouse them from their lowly bed.

For them no more the blazing hearth shall burn,
Or busy housewife ply her evening care:
No children run to lisp their sire's return,
Or climb his knees the envied kiss to share.

... Here rests his head upon the lap of Earth
A youth to Fortune and to Fame unknown.
Fair Science frown'd not on his humble birth,
And Melancholy mark'd him for her own.

Large was his bounty, and his soul sincere,
Heav'n did a recompense as largely send:
He gave to Mis'ry all he had, a tear,
He gain'd from Heav'n ('twas all he wish'd) a friend.

No farther seek his merits to disclose,
Or draw his frailties from their dread abode,
(There they alike in trembling hope repose)
The bosom of his Father and his God.

Epitaph on a Child

POEM

THOMAS GRAY

Here, freed from pain, secure from misery, lies
A child, the darling of his parents' eyes:
A gentler Lamb ne'er sported on the plain,
A fairer flower will never bloom again;
Now let him sleep in peace his night of death.

*Thomas Gray (1716–1771) was an English poet,
classical scholar and professor of history at Cambridge University.*

POEM

Life Goes On

JOYCE GRENFELL

If I should go before the rest of you
Break not a flower
Nor inscribe a stone
Nor when I am gone
Speak in a Sunday voice
But be the usual selves
That I have known

Weep if you must
Parting is hell
But life goes on
So ... sing as well

Joyce Grenfell (1910–1979) was a British comedian and acclaimed wit. She performed comic monologues from 1939 until the early 1950s and later appeared in her own one-woman shows, such as Joyce Grenfell Requests the Pleasure.

The Reassurance

POEM

THOM GUNN

About ten days or so
After we saw you dead
You came back in a dream.
I'm all right now you said.
And it was you, although
You were fleshed out again:
You hugged us all round then,
And gave your welcoming beam.
How like you to be kind,
Seeking to reassure.
And, yes, how like my mind
To make itself secure.

Thom Gunn (1929–2004) was born in Kent but lived most of his life in the United States. He was one of the prominent poets from the generation that included Sylvia Plath and Ted Hughes.

POEM

Remember Me
DAVID HARKINS

You can shed tears that she is gone
Or you can smile because she has lived.

You can close your eyes and pray that she will come back
Or you can open your eyes and see all that she has left.

Your heart can be empty because you can't see her
Or you can be full of the love that you shared.

You can turn your back on tomorrow and live yesterday
Or you can be happy for tomorrow because of yesterday.

You can remember her and only that she is gone
Or you can cherish her memory and let it live on.

You can cry and close your mind, be empty and turn your back
Or you can do what she would want: smile, open your eyes,
love and go on.

*David Harkins (b. 1959) wrote this poem in 1981. It was read at
Elizabeth, the Queen Mother's funeral but was attributed to an anonymous
source. After a lot of press coverage to find the author, Harkins, who is now
a painter in Cumbria, came forward to acknowledge the poem.*

Epitaph Upon a Child that Died

ROBERT HERRICK

POEM

HERE she lies, a pretty bud,
Lately made of flesh and blood;
Who so soon fell fast asleep
As her little eyes did peep.
Give her strewings, but not stir
The earth that lightly covers her.

Robert Herrick (1591–1674) was an English cleric and poet who mixed in literary circles in London with other well known poets, such as Ben Jonson.

POEM

Death Is Nothing at All

HENRY SCOTT HOLLAND

Death is nothing at all,
I have only slipped into the next room
I am I and you are you
Whatever we were to each other, that we are still.
Call me by my old familiar name,
Speak to me in the easy way which you always used
Put no difference in your tone,
Wear no forced air of solemnity or sorrow
Laugh as we always laughed at the little jokes we enjoyed together.
Play, smile, think of me, pray for me.
Let my name be ever the household word that it always was,
Let it be spoken without effect, without the trace of shadow on it.
Life means all that it ever meant.
It is the same as it ever was, there is unbroken continuity.
Why should I be out of mind because I am out of sight?
I am waiting for you, for an interval, somewhere very near,
Just around the corner.
All is well.

Henry Scott Holland (1847–1918) was the Canon of St Paul's Cathedral, London.

from In Our Youth Our Hearts Were Touched By Fire

OLIVER WENDELL HOLMES

... The generation that carried on the war has been
set apart by its experience. Through our great good
fortune, in our youth our hearts were touched with
fire. It was given to us to learn at the outset that life
is a profound and passionate thing. While we are
permitted to scorn nothing but indifference, and do
not pretend to undervalue the worldly rewards of
ambition, we have seen with our own eyes, beyond
and above the gold fields, the snowy heights of honour,
and it is for us to bear the report to those who come
after us. But, above all, we have learned that whether
a man accepts from Fortune her spade, and will look
downward and dig, or from Aspiration her axe and cord,
and will scale the ice, the one and only success which it
is his to command is to bring to his work a mighty heart.

Such hearts – ah me, how many! – were stilled twenty
years ago; and to us who remain behind is left this day
of memories. Every year – in the full tide of spring, at
the height of the symphony of flowers and love and life
– there comes a pause, and through the silence we hear
the lonely pipe of death. Year after year lovers wandering
under the apple trees and through the clover and deep
grass are surprised with sudden tears as they see black

veiled figures stealing through the morning to a soldier's grave. Year after year the comrades of the dead follow, with public honour, procession and commemorative flags and funeral march – honour and grief from us who stand almost alone, and have seen the best and noblest of our generation pass away.

But grief is not the end of all. I seem to hear the funeral march become a paean. I see beyond the forest the moving banners of a hidden column.

Our dead brothers still live for us and bid us think of life, not death – of life to which in their youth they lent the passion and glory of Spring. As I listen, the great chorus of life and joy begins again, and amid the awful orchestra of seen and unseen powers and destinies of good and evil, our trumpets, sound once more a note of daring, hope, and will.

Oliver Wendell Holmes (1809–1894) was an American physician, author and poet best known for his poetry and comic verse. This address was delivered on Memorial Day, 30 May 1884, before the John Sedgwick Post No. 4, Grand Army of the Republic.

Heaven–Haven
[A Nun Takes the Veil]

GERARD MANLEY HOPKINS

POEM

I have desired to go
Where springs not fail,
To fields where flies no sharp and sided hail
And a few lilies blow.

And I have asked to be
Where no storms come,
Where the green swell is in the havens dumb,
And out of the swing of the sea.

79

Gerard Manley Hopkins (1844–89) was a priest and a poet. During the year of his ordination he wrote 11 extraordinary sonnets that expressed his Christian faith. This poem was written in 1918.

POEM

As Befits a Man

LANGSTON HUGHES

I don't mind dying –
But I'd hate to die all alone!
I want a dozen pretty women
To holler, cry, and moan.

I don't mind dying
But I want my funeral to be fine:
A row of long tall mamas
Fainting, fanning, and crying.

I want a fish-tail hearse
And sixteen fish-tail cars,
A big brass band
And a whole truck load of flowers.

When they let me down,
Down into the clay,
I want the women to holler:
Please don't take him away!
Ow-ooo-oo-o!
Don't take daddy away!

Langston Hughes (1902–1967) was an influential African American dramatist and poet who became one of the foremost interpreters to the world of the black experience in the United States.

Wake

LANGSTON HUGHES

POEM

Tell all my mourners
To mourn in red –
Cause there ain't no sense
In my bein' dead ...

*This short poem was first published in Hughes's
volume of poetry, *Shakespeare in Harlem*, in 1942.

Prayer

BEDE JARRETT

We seem to give them back to thee, O God,
who gavest them first to us.
Yet as thou didst not lose them in the giving,
so do we not lose them by their return.
Not as the world giveth, givest thou, O lover of souls.
What thou givest, thou takest not away,
for what is thine is also ours if we are thine.
And life is eternal and love is immortal,
and death is only a horizon,
and a horizon is nothing, save the limit of our sight.
Lift us up, strong Son of God,
that we may see further;
cleanse our eyes that we may see more clearly;
draw us closer to thyself that we may know ourselves
to be nearer to our loved ones who are now with thee.
And while thou dost prepare a place for us,
prepare us also for that happy place,
that where thou art we may also be for evermore.

*Bede Jarrett, (O.P.) (1881–1934) was a Dominican priest living in
England at the beginning of the 20th century. The initials O.P. stand for* Ordo
Prædicatorum *(Order of Preachers), the mendicant religious order founded by St
Dominic in 1215 as part of a monastic reform movement of the Catholic Church.*

I Know that My Redeemer Lives

JOB 19:25-27

BIBLICAL

25 I know that my Redeemer lives, and that in the end
   he will stand upon the earth.
26 And after my skin has been destroyed, yet in my
   flesh I will see God;
27 I myself will see him with my own eyes – I, and not
   another. How my heart yearns within me!

New International Version

83

Jesus Comforts the Sisters

JOHN 11:25-26

BIBLICAL

25 Jesus said to her, 'I am the resurrection and the life.
   He who believes in me will live, even though he dies;
26 and whoever lives and believes in me will never die.
   Do you believe this?'

New International Version

Candle in the Wind*

ELTON JOHN

Goodbye England's rose;
may you ever grow in our hearts.
You were the grace that placed itself
where lives were torn apart.
You called out to our country,
and you whispered to those in pain.
Now you belong to heaven,
and the stars spell out your name.

And it seems to me you lived your life
like a candle in the wind:
never fading with the sunset
when the rain set in.
And your footsteps will always fall here,
along England's greenest hills;
your candle's burned out long before
your legend ever will.

Loveliness we've lost;
these empty days without your smile.
This torch we'll always carry
for our nation's golden child.
And even though we try,
the truth brings us to tears;
all our words cannot express
the joy you brought us through the years.

Goodbye England's rose,
from a country lost without your soul,
who'll miss the wings of your compassion
more than you'll ever know.

*Originally written in 1973, this song (music by Sir Elton John and
lyrics by Bernie Taupin) was composed in honour of the iconic actor
Marilyn Monroe and appeared on Elton John's best-selling album
Goodbye Yellow Brick Road. When Princess Diana, former wife of
Prince Charles, heir to the British throne, died in 1997, John, a close
friend, adapted the words with Taupin to suit Diana, 'the English Rose'
and performed it at her funeral in Westminster Abbey, London.

85

*Sir Elton John (b. 1947) is a singer, composer and pianist and
remains one of the most popular entertainers of the late 20th and
early 21st century.*

POEM

On My First Son

BEN JONSON

Farewell, thou child of my right hand, and joy;
My sin was too much hope of thee, lov'd boy.
Seven years thou wert lent to me, and I thee pay.
Exacted by the fate, on the just day.
Oh, could I lose all father now! For why
Will man lament the state he should envy?
To have so soon 'scaped world's and flesh's rage,
And, if no other misery, yet age?
Rest in soft peace, and asked, say here doth lie
Ben Jonson his best piece of poetry;
For whose sake, henceforth, all his vows be such,
As what he loves may never like too much.

Ben Jonson (1572–1637) was a Jacobean playwright best known for his satirical and witty comedies such as Volpone. *He was part of a group of writers who gathered at the Mermaid tavern in Cheapside, London, and had a great influence on younger writers. He wrote this poem following the death of his son.*

Memory of My Father

POEM

PATRICK KAVANAGH

Every old man I see
Reminds me of my father
When he had fallen in love with death
One time when sheaves were gathered.

That man I saw in Gardner Street
Stumble on the kerb was one,
He stared at me half-eyed,
I might have been his son.

And I remember the musician
Faltering over his fiddle
In Bayswater, London,
He too set me the riddle.

Every old man I see
In October-coloured weather
Seems to say to me:
'I was once your father.'

Patrick Kavanagh (1904–1967) was an Irish poet and writer. His epic poem, 'The Great Hunger', placed him in the front rank of modern Irish poets.

I Had a Dove, and the Sweet Dove Died

JOHN KEATS

I had a dove, and the sweet dove died,
And I have thought it died of grieving;
O what could it grieve for? Its feet were tied
With a silken thread of my own hand's weaving:
Sweet little red feet! Why would you die?
Why would you leave me, sweet bird, why?
You liv'd alone on the forest tree,
Why, pretty thing, could you not live with me?
I kiss'd you oft, and gave you white pease;
Why not live sweetly as in the green trees?

John Keats (1795–1821) was a leading figure in the Romantic Movement. He died of consumption in Rome, aged 26. Despite the brevity of his life, Keats' poems created a landmark in English poetry.

Ode: 'Bards of Passion and of Mirth'

POEM

JOHN KEATS

Bards of Passion and of Mirth,
Ye have left your souls on earth!
Have ye souls in heaven too,
Double lived in regions new?
Yes, and those of heaven commune
With the spheres of sun and moon;
With the noise of fountains wound'rous,
And the parle of voices thund'rous;
With the whisper of heaven's trees
And one another, in soft ease.

Seated on Elysian lawns
Brows'd by none but Dian's fawns;
Underneath large blue-bells tented,
Where the daisies are rose-scented,
And the rose herself has got
Perfume which on earth is not;
Where the nightingale doth sing
Not a senseless, tranced thing,
But divine melodious truth;
Philosophic numbers smooth;
Tales and golden histories
Of heaven and its mysteries.

Thus ye live on high, and then
On the earth ye live again;
And the souls ye left behind you
Teach us, here, the way to find you,
Where your other souls are joying,
Never slumber'd, never cloying.
Here, your earth-born souls still speak
To mortals, of their little week;
Of their sorrows and delights;
Of their passions and their spites;
Of their glory and their shame;
What doth strengthen and what maim.
Thus ye teach us, every day,
Wisdom, though fled far away.

Bards of Passion and of Mirth,
Ye have left your souls on earth!
Ye have souls in heaven too,
Double-lived in regions new!

To Sleep

JOHN KEATS

O soft embalmer of the still midnight,
Shutting, with careful
fingers and benign,
Our gloom-pleas'd eyes,
embower'd from the light,
Enshaded in forgetfulness divine:
O soothest Sleep! if so it please thee, close
In midst of this thine hymn my willing eyes,
Or wait the 'Amen,' ere thy poppy throws
Around my bed its lulling charities.
Then save me, or the passed day will shine
Upon my pillow, breeding many woes,–
Save me from curious Conscience,
that still lords
Its strength for darkness,
burrowing like a mole;
Turn the key deftly
in the oiled wards,
And seal the hushed
Casket of my Soul.

From Blossoms

LI-YOUNG LEE

From blossoms comes
this brown paper bag of peaches
we bought from the boy
at the bend in the road where we turned toward
signs painted Peaches.

From laden boughs, from hands
from sweet fellowship in the bins,
comes nectar at the roadside, succulent
peaches we devour, dusty skin and all,
comes the familiar dust of summer, dust we eat.

O, to take what we love inside,
to carry within us an orchard, to eat
not only the skin, but the shade,
not only the sugar, but the days, to hold
the fruit in our hands, adore it, then bite into
the round jubilance of peach.

There are days we live
as if death were nowhere
in the background; from joy
to joy to joy, from wing to wing,
from blossom to blossom to
impossible blossom, to sweet impossible blossom.

Li-Young Lee (b. 1957) was born in Indonesia to Chinese parents.
His family settled in America after they were forced to escape anti-Chinese
persecution. He lives in Chicago and has won several awards for his work.

from A Grief Observed

C.S. LEWIS

... No-one ever told me that grief felt so much like fear. I am not afraid, but the sensation is like being afraid. The same fluttering in the stomach, the same restlessness, the yawning. I keep swallowing.

At other times it feels like being mildly drunk, or concussed. There is a sort of invisible blanket between the world and me. I find it hard to take in what anyone says. Or perhaps, hard to want to take it in. It is so uninteresting. Yet I want the others to be about me. I dread the moments when the house is empty. If only they could talk to one another and not to me.

There are moments, most unexpectedly, when something inside me tries to assure me that I really don't mind so much, not so very much at all. Love is not the whole of a man's life. I was happy before I met H. I've plenty of what are called 'resources'. People get over these things. Come, I shan't do so badly. One is ashamed to listen to this voice but it seems for a little to be making out a good case. Then comes a sudden jab of red-hot memory and all this 'commonsense' vanishes like an ant in the mouth of a furnace ...

Clive Staple Lewis (1895–1963), *or 'Jack' as he was known to his friends and family, is probably best known for writing the Narnia series. An Oxford don, Lewis married Joy Davidman and wrote* A Grief Observed *after her tragic death in 1960.*

LETTER

from Letter to Mrs Bixby

ABRAHAM LINCOLN

... I pray that our Heavenly Father may assuage the anguish of your bereavement, and leave you only the cherished memory of the loved and lost, and the solemn pride that must be yours, to have laid so costly a sacrifice upon the altar of Freedom.

Abraham Lincoln (1809–1865) was the 16th President of the United States. He wrote this letter on 21 November 1864 to Mrs Lydia Bixby, a widow who is thought to have lost five sons in the Civil War (1861–1865). It was later printed in the Boston Evening Transcript.

Farewell

POEM

FEDERICO GARCÍA LORCA

If I die,
leave the balcony open.

The little boy is eating oranges.
(From my balcony I can see him.)

The reaper is harvesting the wheat.
(From my balcony I can hear him.)

If I die,
leave the balcony open!

Federico García Lorca (1898–1936) was one of the most popular poets of the Spanish-speaking world and one of the most powerful dramatists in the modern theatre. He was assassinated in August 1936 by General Franco's Nationalists during the Spanish Civil War (1936–1939).

POEM

Abide With Me

H.F. LYTE

Abide with me; fast falls the eventide;
The darkness deepens; Lord with me abide.
When other helpers fail and comforts flee,
Help of the helpless, O abide with me.

Swift to its close ebbs out life's little day;
Earth's joys grow dim; its glories pass away;
Change and decay in all around I see;
O Thou who changest not, abide with me.

Not a brief glance I beg, a passing word,
But as Thou dwell'st with Thy disciples, Lord,
Familiar, condescending, patient, free.
Come not to sojourn, but abide with me.

Come not in terrors, as the King of kings,
But kind and good, with healing in Thy wings;
Tears for all woes, a heart for every plea.
Come, Friend of sinners, thus abide with me.

Thou on my head in early youth didst smile,
And though rebellious and perverse meanwhile,
Thou hast not left me, oft as I left Thee.
On to the close, O Lord, abide with me.

I need Thy presence every passing hour.
What but Thy grace can foil the tempter's power?
Who, like Thyself, my guide and stay can be?
Through cloud and sunshine, Lord, abide with me.

I fear no foe, with Thee at hand to bless;
Ills have no weight, and tears no bitterness.
Where is death's sting? Where, grave, thy victory?
I triumph still, if Thou abide with me.

Hold Thou Thy cross before my closing eyes;
Shine through the gloom and point me to the skies.
Heaven's morning breaks, and earth's vain shadows flee;
In life, in death, O Lord, abide with me.

H.F. Lyte (1793–1847) wrote this hymn when he was dying of tuberculosis and finished it the Sunday he gave his farewell sermon to his parish. He died in France three weeks later and the bells of his church at All Saints in Lower Brixham, Devonshire, have rung out 'Abide With Me' daily since his death.

POEM

Of You

NORMAN MACCAIG

When the little devil, panic,
begins to grin and jump about
in my heart, in my brain, in my muscles,
I am shown the path I had lost
in the mountainy mist.

I'm writing of you.

When the pain that will kill me
is about to be unbearable,
a cool hand
puts a tablet on my tongue and the pain
dwindles away and vanishes.

I'm writing of you.

There are fires to be suffered,
the blaze of cruelty, the smolder
of inextinguishable longing, even
the gentle candleflame of peace
that burns too.

I suffer them. I survive.

I'm writing of you.

*Norman MacCaig (1910–1969) was a Scottish poet, known
for his humour and the simplicity of his language.*

Meeting Point

LOUIS MACNEICE

POEM

Time was away and somewhere else,
There were two glasses and two chairs
And two people with the one pulse
(Somebody stopped the moving stairs)
Time was away and somewhere else.

And they were neither up nor down;
The stream's music did not stop
Flowing through heather, limpid brown,
Although they sat in a coffee shop
And they were neither up nor down.

The bell was silent in the air
Holding its inverted poise –
Between the clang and clang a flower,
A brazen calyx of no noise:
The bell was silent in the air.

The camels crossed the miles of sand
That stretched around the cups and plates;
The desert was their own, they planned
To portion out the stars and dates:
The camels crossed the miles of sand.

Time was away and somewhere else.
The waiter did not come, the clock
Forgot them and the radio waltz
Came out like water from a rock:
Time was away and somewhere else.

Her fingers flicked away the ash
That bloomed again in tropic trees:
Not caring if the markets crash
When they had forests such as these,
Her fingers flicked away the ash.

God or whatever means the Good
Be praised that time can stop like this,
That what the heart has understood
Can verify in the body's peace
God or whatever means the Good.

Time was away and she was here
And life no longer what it was,
The bell was silent in the air
And all the room one glow because
Time was away and she was here.

Louis MacNeice (1907–1963) was a Belfast-born poet. A friend and contemporary of W. H. Auden and Stephen Spender at Oxford, he closely collaborated with the leftwing poets of the 1930s.

In Flanders Fields

JOHN McCRAE

In Flanders fields the poppies blow
Between the crosses, row on row,
That mark our place; and in the sky
The larks, still bravely singing, fly
Scarce heard amid the guns below.
We are the Dead. Short days ago
We lived, felt dawn, saw sunset glow,
Loved and were loved, and now we lie
In Flanders fields.
Take up our quarrel with the foe:
To you from failing hands we throw
The torch; be yours to hold it high.
If ye break faith with us who die
We shall not sleep, though poppies grow
In Flanders fields.

Lieutenant-Colonel John McCrae (1872–1918) wrote this poem in 1915 during the First World War (1914–1918). It commemorates the deaths of the thousands of young men who died in Flanders and is inspired by the blood-red poppies that bloomed in the fields where many of his friends had died.

High Flight

JOHN GILLESPIE MCGEE

Oh, I have slipped the surly bonds of earth
And danced the skies on laughter-silvered wings.
Sunward I've climbed and joined the tumbling mirth
Of sun split clouds – and done a hundred things
You have not dreamed of; wheeled and soared and swung
High in the sunlit silence. Hovering there
I've chased the shouting wind along, and flung
My eager craft through footless halls of air;
Up, up the long delirious burning blue
I've topped the windswept heights with easy grace,
Where never lark nor even eagle flew;
And while, with silent lifting mind I've trod
The high, untrespassed sanctity of space
Put out my hand and touched the face of God.

*Flight Officer John Gillespie McGee (1922–1941) wrote this
when he was 19, just weeks before his death. Loved by aviators and pilots,
it was also quoted by President Ronald Reagan (1911–2004) in his broadcast
to the US nation following the* Challenger *shuttle disaster in 1986.*

An Epitaph

POEM

WALTER DE LA MARE

Here lies a most beautiful lady,
Light of step and heart was she:
I think she was the most beautiful lady
That ever was in the West Country.
But beauty vanishes; beauty passes;
However rare, rare it be;
And when I crumble who shall remember
This lady of the West Country?

Walter de la Mare (1873–1956) was a poet and writer. He was a relative of the Victorian poet Robert Browning.

POEM

Dirge Without Music

EDNA ST VINCENT MILLAY

I am not resigned to the shutting away of loving hearts in the
hard ground.
So it is, and so it will be, for so it has been, time out of mind:
Into the darkness they go, the wise and the lovely. Crowned
With lilies and with laurel they go; but I am not resigned.

Lovers and thinkers, into the earth with you.
Be one with the dull, the indiscriminate dust.
A fragment of what you felt, of what you knew,
A formula, a phrase remains, – but the rest is lost.

The answer quick and keen, the honest look, the laughter,
the love,–
They are gone. They have gone to feed the roses. Elegant
and curled
Is the blossom. Fragrant is the blossom. I know. But I do
not approve.
More precious was the light in your eyes than all roses in
the world.

Down, down, down into the darkness of the grave
Gently they go, the beautiful, the tender, the kind;
Quietly they go, the intelligent, the witty, the brave.
I know. But I do not approve. And I am not resigned.

*Edna St Vincent Millay (1892–1950) was an American playwright
and lyrical poet.*

from The House at Pooh Corner

NOVEL

A . A .   M I L N E

... Then, suddenly again, Christopher Robin, who
was still looking at the world with his chin in his hands,
called out 'Pooh!'

'Yes?' said Pooh.

'When I'm – when – Pooh!'

'Yes, Christopher Robin?'

'I'm not going to do Nothing any more.'

'Never again?'

'Well, not so much. They don't let you.'

Pooh waited for him to go on, but he was silent again.

'Yes, Christopher Robin?' said Pooh helpfully.

'Pooh, when I'm – you know – when I'm not doing
Nothing, will you come up here sometimes?'

'Just Me?'

'Yes, Pooh.'

'Will you be here too?'

'Yes, Pooh, I will be really. I promise I will
be, Pooh.'

'That's good,' said Pooh.

'Pooh, promise you won't forget about me, ever.
Not even when I'm a hundred.'

Pooh thought for a little.

'How old shall I be then?'

'Ninety-nine.'

Pooh nodded.

'I promise,' he said.

Still with his eyes on the world Christopher Robin put out a hand and felt for Pooh's paw.

'Pooh,' said Christopher Robin earnestly, 'if I – if I'm not quite' he stopped and tried again – 'Pooh, whatever happens you will understand, won't you?'

'Understand what?'

'Oh, nothing.' He laughed and jumped to his feet. 'Come on!'

'Where?' said Pooh.

'Anywhere,' said Christopher Robin.

So they went off together. But wherever they go, and whatever happens to them on the way, in that enchanted place on the top of the Forest a little boy and his Bear will always be playing.

A.A. Milne (1892–1956) was a humourist and playwright. He is probably best known for creating the characters Winnie the Pooh and Christopher Robin. This passage is taken from Chapter 10 of The House at Pooh Corner *(1928) in which Christopher and Pooh come to an enchanted place and we leave them there.*

I am Not Alone

GABRIELA MISTRAL

POEM

The night, it is deserted
from the mountains to the sea.
But I, the one who rocks you,
I am not alone!

The sky, it is deserted
for the moon falls to the sea.
But I, the one who holds you,
I am not alone!

The world, it is deserted.
All flesh is sad you see.
But I, the one who hugs you,
I am not alone!

*Gabriela Mistral (1889–1957) was the first Latin American
poet to receive the Nobel Prize for Literature.*

Eulogy to Mahatma Gandhi*

JAWAHARLAL NEHRU

Friends and Comrades,

The light has gone out of our lives and there is darkness everywhere. I do not know what to tell you and how to say it. Our beloved leader, Bapu as we call him, the Father of the Nation, is no more. Perhaps I am wrong to say that. Nevertheless, we will not see him again as we have seen him for these many years. We will not run to him for advice and seek solace from him, and that is a terrible blow, not to me only but to millions and millions of this country. And it is a little more difficult to soften the blow by any other advice that I or anyone else can give you.

The light has gone out, I said, and yet I was wrong. For the light that shone in our country was no ordinary light. The light that has illumined this country for these many many years will illumine this country for many more years, and a thousand years later that light will still be seen in this country and the world will see it and it will give solace to innumerable hearts. For that light represented something more than the immediate present; it represented the living, the eternal truths, reminding us of the right path, drawing us from error, taking this ancient country to freedom.

All this has happened when there was so much more for him to do. We could never think that he was unnecessary or that he had done his task. But now, particularly, when we are faced with so many difficulties, his not being with us is a blow most terrible to bear ...

... we should, in strength and in unity, face all the troubles that are in front of us. We must hold together, and all our petty troubles and difficulties and conflicts must be ended in the face of its great disaster. A great disaster is a symbol to us to remember all the big things of life and forget the small things of which we have thought too much. In his death he has reminded us of the big things of life, the living truth ...

*Mahatma Gandhi (1869–1948) was the spiritual leader of India. A nationalist, often referred to as 'Bapu' by his followers, he led passive resistance movements in both South Africa and India, protesting against unequal treatment of native populations by the British. Under his guidance, India became independent on 15 August 1947. He was assassinated by a Muslim on 30 January 1948.

Jawaharlal Nehru (1889–1964) was a leading Indian nationalist leader and the first prime minister of independent India (1947). The above extract is from his public announcement of Gandhi's assassination on 30 January 1948.

POEM

Song of Despair

PABLO NERUDA

The memory of you emerges from the night around me.
The river mingles its stubborn lament with the sea.

Deserted like the dwarves at dawn.
It is the hour of departure, oh deserted one!

Cold flower heads are raining over my heart.
Oh pit of debris, fierce cave of the shipwrecked.

In you the wars and the flights accumulated.
From you the wings of the song birds rose.

You swallowed everything, like distance.
Like the sea, like time. In you everything sank!

It was the happy hour of assault and the kiss.
The hour of the spell that blazed like a lighthouse.

Pilot's dread, fury of blind driver,
turbulent drunkenness of love, in you everything sank!

In the childhood of mist my soul, winged and wounded.
Lost discoverer, in you everything sank!

You girdled sorrow, you clung to desire,
sadness stunned you, in you everything sank!

I made the wall of shadow draw back,
beyond desire and act, I walked on.

Oh flesh, my own flesh, woman whom I loved and lost,
I summon you in the moist hour, I raise my song to you.

Like a jar you housed infinite tenderness.
and the infinite oblivion shattered you like a jar.

There was the black solitude of the islands,
and there, woman of love, your arms took me in.

There was thirst and hunger, and you were the fruit.
There were grief and ruins, and you were the miracle.

Ah woman, I do not know how you could contain me
in the earth of your soul, in the cross of your arms!

How terrible and brief my desire was to you!
How difficult and drunken, how tensed and avid.

Cemetery of kisses, there is still fire in your tombs,
still the fruited boughs burn, pecked at by birds.

Oh the bitten mouth, oh the kissed limbs,
oh the hungering teeth, oh the entwined bodies.

Oh the mad coupling of hope and force
in which we merged and despaired.

And the tenderness, light as water and as flour.
And the word scarcely begun on the lips.

This was my destiny and in it was my voyage of my longing,
and in it my longing fell, in you everything sank!

Oh pit of debris, everything fell into you,
what sorrow did you not express, in what sorrow are you not
drowned!

From billow to billow you still called and sang.
Standing like a sailor in the prow of a vessel.

You still flowered in songs, you still brike the currents.
Oh pit of debris, open and bitter well.

Pale blind diver, luckless slinger,
lost discoverer, in you everything sank!

It is the hour of departure, the hard cold hour
which the night fastens to all the timetables.

The rustling belt of the sea girdles the shore.
Cold stars heave up, black birds migrate.

Deserted like the wharves at dawn.
Only tremulous shadow twists in my hands.

Oh farther than everything. Oh farther than everything.
It is the hour of departure. Oh abandoned one!

Pablo Neruda (1904–1973) was a Nobel prize-winning Chilean poet. His love poetry captured the imagination of the world: the volume Twenty Love Songs and a Song of Despair *from which this poem is taken has sold over one million copies.*

Sonnet LXXXIX

PABLO NERUDA

POEM

When I die, I want your hands on my eyes:
I want the light and the wheat of your beloved hands
to pass their freshness over me once more:
I want to feel the softness that changed my destiny.

I want you to live while I wait for you, asleep.
I want your ears still to hear the wind, I want you
to sniff the sea's aroma that we loved together,
to continue to walk on the sand we walk on.

I want what I love to continue to live,
and you whom I love and sang above everything else
to continue to flourish, full-flowered:

so that you can reach everything my love directs you to,
so that my shadow can travel along in your hair,
so that everything can learn the reason for my song.

The Serenity Prayer

REINHOLD NIEBUHR

God, give us grace to accept with serenity
the things that cannot be changed,
Courage to change the things
which should be changed,
and the Wisdom to distinguish
the one from the other.

Living one day at a time,
Enjoying one moment at a time,
Accepting hardship as a pathway to peace,
Taking, as Jesus did,
This sinful world as it is,
Not as I would have it,
Trusting that You will make all things right,
If I surrender to Your will,
So that I may be reasonably happy in this life,
And supremely happy with You forever in the next.

Amen.

*Reinhold Niebuhr (1892–1921) was an American Protestant theologian.
He wrote several influential books on religion.*

Stanzas 21–31 from The Rubáiyát of Omar Khayyám

OMAR KHAYYÁM

Lo! some we loved, the loveliest and best
That Time and Fate of all their Vintage prest,
Have drunk their Cup a Round or two before,
And one by one crept silently to Rest.

And we, that now make merry in the Room
They left, and Summer dresses in new Bloom,
Ourselves must we beneath a Couch of Earth
Descend, ourselves to make a Couch – for whom?

Ah, make the most of what we yet may spend,
Before we too into Dust descend;
Dust into Dust, and under Dust, to lie
Sans Wine, sans Song, sans Singer, and – sans End!

Alike for those who for TO-DAY prepare,
And those that after a TO-MORROW stare,
A Muezzín from the Tower of Darkness cries
'Fools! your Reward is neither Here not There!'

Why, all the Saints and Sages who discuss'd
Of the Two Worlds so learnedly, are thrust
Like foolish Prophets forth; their Words to Scorn
Are scatter'd, and their Mouths are stopt with Dust.

Oh, come with old Khayyám, and leave the Wise
To talk; one thing is certain, that Life flies;
One thing is certain, and the Rest is Lies;
The Flower that once has blown for ever dies.

Myself when young did eagerly frequent
Doctor and Saint, and heard great Argument
About it and about: but evermore
Came out by the same Door as in I went.

With them the Seed of Wisdom did I sow,
And with my own hand labour'd it to grow:
And this was all the Harvest that I reap'd –
'I came like Water, and like Wind I go.'

Into this Universe, and why not knowing,
Nor whence, like Water willy-nilly flowing:
And out of it, as Wind along the Waste
I know not whither, willy-nilly blowing.

What, without asking, hither hurried whence?
And, without asking, whither hurried hence!
Another and another Cup to drown
The Memory of this Impertinence.

Up from Earth's Centre through the Seventh Gate
I rose, and on the Throne of Saturn sate,
And many Knots unravel'd by the Road;
But not the Knot of Human Death and Fate.

Omar Khayyám (1048–1122) was an Islamic scholar in Iran who was a poet and mathematician. He compiled astronomical tables, contributed to calendar reform and discovered a geometrical method of solving cubic equations by intersecting a parabola with a circle. He is best known for his poetry.

Anthem for Doomed Youth*

POEM

WILFRED OWEN

What passing-bells for these who die as cattle?
– Only the monstruous anger of the guns.
Only the stuttering rifles' rapid rattle
Can patter out their hasty orisons.
No mockeries now for them; no prayers nor bells;
Nor any voice of mourning save the choirs, –
The shrill, demented choirs of wailing shells;
And bugles calling for them from sad shires.

What candles may be held to speed them all?
Not in the hands of boys, but in their eyes
Shall shine the holy glimmers of good-byes.
The pallor of girls' brows shall be their pall;
Their flowers the tenderness of patient minds,
And each slow dusk a drawing-down of blinds.

117

*This poem was written between September and October 1918.

Wilfred Owen (1893–1918) was a British poet, primarily known for his war poetry, like his great friend Siegfried Sassoon. Owen died on 4 November 1918 in one of the last battles of the First World War (1914–1918). The Armistice bells rang just a week later on 11 November 1918 proclaiming the end of the war.

POEM

Greater Love

WILFRED OWEN

Red lips are not so red
As the stained stones kissed by the English dead.
Kindness of wooed and wooer
Seems shame to their love pure.
O Love, your eyes lose lure
When I behold eyes blinded in my stead!

Your slender attitude
Trembles not exquisite like limbs knife-skewed,
Rolling and rolling there
Where God seems not to care;
Till the fierce Love they bear
Cramps them in death's extreme decrepitude.

Your voice sings not so soft, –
Though even as wind murmuring through raftered loft, –
Your dear voice is not dear,
Gentle, and evening clear,
As theirs whom none now hear
Now earth has stopped their piteous mouths that coughed.

Heart, you were never hot,
Nor large, nor full like hearts made great with shot;
And though your hand be pale,
Paler are all which trail
Your cross through flame and hail:
Weep, you may weep, for you may touch them not.

But Not Forgotten

DOROTHY PARKER

POEM

I think no matter where you stray,
That I shall go with you a way.
Though you may wander sweeter lands,
You will not forget my hands,
Nor yet the way I held my head
Nor the tremulous things I said.
You will still see me, small and white
And smiling, in the secret night,
And feel my arms about you when
The day comes fluttering back again.
I think, no matter where you be,
You'll hold me in your memory
And keep my image there without me,
By telling later loves about me.

Dorothy Parker (1893–1967) was an American writer and satirist who held court at the Algonquin Hotel in New York.

POEM

Coda

DOROTHY PARKER

There's little in taking or giving,
There's little in water or wine;
This living, this living, this living
Was never a project of mine.
Oh, hard is the struggle, and sparse is
The gain of the one at the top,
For art is a form of catharsis,
And love is a permanent flop,
And work is the province of cattle,
And rest's for a clam in a shell,
So I'm thinking of throwing the battle —
Would you kindly direct me to hell?

120

The Moon and the Yew Tree

POEM

SYLVIA PLATH

This is the light of the mind, cold and planetary
The trees of the mind are black. The light is blue.
The grasses unload their griefs on my feet as if I were God
Prickling my ankles and murmuring of their humility
Fumy, spiritous mists inhabit this place.
Separated from my house by a row of headstones.
I simply cannot see where there is to get to.

The moon is no door. It is a face in its own right,
White as a knuckle and terribly upset.
It drags the sea after it like a dark crime; it is quiet
With the O-gape of complete despair. I live here.
Twice on Sunday, the bells startle the sky –
Eight great tongues affirming the Resurrection
At the end, they soberly bong out their names.

The yew tree points up, it has a Gothic shape.
The eyes lift after it and find the moon.
The moon is my mother. She is not sweet like Mary.
Her blue garments unloose small bats and owls.
How I would like to believe in tenderness –
The face of the effigy, gentled by candles,
Bending, on me in particular, its mild eyes.

I have fallen a long way. Clouds are flowering
Blue and mystical over the face of the stars
Inside the church, the saints will all be blue,
Floating on their delicate feet over the cold pews,
Their hands and faces stiff with holiness.
The moon sees nothing of this. She is bald and wild.

Sylvia Plath (1932–1963) was a leading American poet who was married to fellow poet Ted Hughes. Plath committed suicide after several unsuccessful attempts at the age of 31. Her poetry and life has been the subject of many studies and films.

from Plutarch's Letters

PLUTARCH

... The soul, being eternal, after death is like a caged bird that has been released. If it has been a long time in the body, and has become tame by many affairs and long habit, the soul will immediately take another body and once again become involved in the troubles of the world. The worst thing about old age is that the soul's memory of the other world grows dim, while at the same time its attachment to things of this world becomes so strong that the soul tends to retain the form that it had in the body. But that soul which remains only a short time within a body, until liberated by the higher powers, quickly recovers its fire and goes on to higher things.

Plutarch (c. AD 46–120) was a leading Greek historian and philosopher. He wrote this letter to his wife after the death of their two-year-old daughter.

BIBLICAL

The Lord Is My Shepherd

PSALM 23

1 The LORD is my shepherd, I shall not be in want.
2 He makes me lie down in green pastures, he leads me
   beside quiet waters,
3 He restores my soul. He guides me in paths of righteousness
   for his name's sake.
4 Even though I walk through the valley of the shadow of
   death, I will fear no evil, for you are with me; your rod
   and your staff, they comfort me.
5 You prepare a table before me in the presence of my enemies.
   You anoint my head with oil; my cup overflows.
6 Surely goodness and love will follow me all the days of my
   life, and I will dwell in the house of the LORD forever.

New International Version

BIBLICAL

God Is Our Refuge

PSALM 46:1-4

1 God is our refuge and strength, an ever-present help
   in trouble.
2 Therefore we will not fear, though the earth give way
   and the mountains fall into the heart of the sea,
3 though its waters roar and foam and the mountains
   quake with their surging.
4 There is a river whose streams make glad the city of
   God, the holy place where the Most High dwells.

New International Version

White Ashes

R E N N Y O   S H O N I N

... When I deeply contemplate the transient nature of human life, I realize that, from beginning to end, life is impermanent like an illusion. We have not yet heard of anyone who lived ten thousand years. How fleeting is a lifetime!

Who in this world today can maintain a human form for even a hundred years?

There is no knowing whether I will die first or others, whether death will occur today or tomorrow. We depart one after another more quickly than the dewdrops on the roots or the tips of the blades of grasses. So it is said. Hence, we may have radiant faces in the morning, but by evening we may turn into white ashes.Once the winds of impermanence have blown, our eyes are instantly closed and our breath stops forever. Then, our radiant face changes its colour, and the attractive countenance like peach and plum blossoms is lost. Family and relatives will gather and grieve, but all to no avail?

Since there is nothing else that can be done, they carry the deceased out to the fields, and then what is left after the body has been cremated and has turned into the midnight smoke is just white ashes. Words fail to describe the sadness of it all.

Thus the ephemeral nature of human existence is such that death comes to young and old alike without discrimination. So we should all quickly take to heart the matter of the greatest importance of the afterlife, entrust ourselves deeply to Amida Buddha, and recite the nembutsu. Humbly and respectfully.

Rennyo Shonin (1415–1499) was a Japanese Buddhist leader and patriarch of the Hongan Temple in Kyÿto. He helped the Buddhist reform that created the Jÿdo Shinsh ('True Pure Land Sect') and inspired the Ikkÿ rebellions, the 15th-century uprisings by militant Buddhists against Japanese feudal lords.

The Great Multitude in White Robes

REVELATION 7:9–17

9   After this I looked and there before me was a
    great multitude that no one could count, from
    every nation, tribe, people and language, standing
    before the throne and in front of the Lamb. They
    were wearing white robes and were holding palm
    branches in their hands.

10 And they cried out in a loud voice: 'Salvation
    belongs to our God, who sits on the throne, and
    to the Lamb.'

11 All the angels were standing around the throne
    and around the elders and the four living creatures.
    They fell down on their faces before the throne
    and worshipped God,

12 saying: 'Amen! Praise and glory and wisdom
    and thanks and honour and power and strength
    be to our God for ever and ever. Amen!'

13 Then one of the elders asked me, 'These in
    white robes – who are they, and where did they
    come from?'

14 I answered, 'Sir, you know. And he said, 'These
    are they who have come out of the great tribulation;
    they have washed their robes and made them white
    in the blood of the Lamb.'

15 Therefore, 'they are before the throne of God and
   serve him day and night in his temple; and he who
   sits on the throne will spread his tent over them.
16 Never again will they hunger; never again will
   they thirst. The sun will not beat upon them,
   nor any scorching heat.
17 For the Lamb at the centre of the throne will
   be their shepherd; he will lead them to springs of
   living water. And God will wipe away every tear
   from their eyes.'

New International Version

The Three Angels
REVELATION 14:13

13 Then I heard a voice from heaven say, 'Write:
   Blessed are the dead who die in the Lord from now
   on.' 'Yes,' says the Spirit, 'they will rest from their
   labour, for their deeds will follow them.'

New International Version

BIBLICAL

The New Jerusalem

REVELATION 21:1—4

1   Then I saw a new heaven and a new earth, for the
     first heaven and the first earth had passed away, and
     there was no longer any sea.
2   I saw the Holy City, the new Jerusalem, coming down
     out of heaven from God, prepared as a bride beautifully
     dressed for her husband.
3   And I heard a loud voice from the throne saying,
     'Now the dwelling of God is with men, and he will live
     with them. They will be his people, and God himself will
     be with them and be their God.
4   He will wipe every tear from their eyes. There will be
     no more death or mourning or crying or pain, for the
     old order of things has passed away.'

New International Version

More Than Conquerors

37 No, in all these things we are more than conquerors
through him who loved us.
38 For I am convinced that neither death nor life, neither
angels nor demons, neither the present nor the future,
nor any powers,
39 Neither height nor depth, nor anything else in all
creation, will be able to separate us from the love of
God that is in Christ Jesus our Lord.

New International Version

POEM

Remember Me When I am Gone

CHRISTINA ROSSETTI

Remember me when I am gone away,
Gone far away into the silent land:
When you can no more hold me by the hand,
Nor I half turn to go yet turning stay.
Remember me when no more day by day
You tell me of our future that you planned:
Only remember me; you understand
It will be late to counsel then or pray.
Yet if you should forget me for a while
And afterwards remember, do not grieve:
For if the darkness and corruption leave
A vestige of the thoughts that once I had,
Better by far you should forget and smile
Than that you should remember and be sad.

Christina Rossetti (1830–1894) came from a very talented family and is viewed as one of the most important female poets of 19th century England. She was a devout evangelical Christian and her poetry often deals with themes such as God, mankind, death, love and metaphysics.

Song

CHRISTINA ROSSETTI

When I am dead my dearest,
Sing no sad songs for me;
Plant thou no roses at my head,
Nor shady cypress tree:
Be the green grass above me
With showers and dewdrops wet;
And if thou wilt, remember,
And if thou wilt, forget.

I shall not see the shadows,
I shall not feel the rain;
I shall not hear the nightingale
Sing on as if in pain:
And dreaming through the twilight
That doth not rise nor set,
Haply I may remember,
And haply may forget.

POEM ## from Fountain of Fire[*]

JALALUD'DIN RUMI

you mustn't be afraid of death
you're a deathless soul
you can't be kept in a dark grave
you're filled with God's glow

be happy with your beloved
you can't find any better
the world will shimmer
because of the diamond you hold

when your heart is immersed
in this blissful love
you can easily endure
any bitter face around

in the absence of malice
there is nothing but
happiness and good times
don't dwell in sorrow my friend

[*]Translated by Nader Khalili

Jalalud'din Rumi (1207–1273) was a philosopher, mystic, scholar, poet and founder of the Whirling Dervishes, a spiritual offshoot of Islam. His poetry centres on the themes of tolerance, goodness, the experience of God, charity and awareness through love.

Why Cling*

JELALUD'DIN RUMI

Why cling to one life
till it is soiled and ragged?

The sun dies and dies
squandering a hundred lived
every instant

God has decreed life for you
and He will give
another and another and another

*Translated by Daniel Liebert

A Prayer for Peace

ST FRANCIS OF ASSISI

Make me a channel of your peace.
Where there is hatred, let us sow love;
Where there is injury, your pardon;
Where there is discord, union;
Where there is doubt, faith;
Where there is despair, hope;
Where there is darkness, light;
Where there is sadness, joy;
O divine master, grant that we may not so much seek
To be consoled as to console,
To be understood as to understand,
To be loved as to love,
For it is in giving that we receive,
It is in pardoning that we are pardoned;
And it is in dying that we are born to eternal life.

Amen.

St Francis of Assisi (1182–1226) was born into a wealthy merchant family and enjoyed an extravagant youth before he devoted himself to God. He spent the rest of his life helping the poor, preaching, praying and serving God.

from The Little Prince

A N T O I N E D E S A I N T - E X U P É R Y

'All men have the stars,' he answered, 'but they are not
the same things for different people. For some, who are
travellers, the stars are guides. For others they are no
more than little lights in the sky. For others, who are
scholars, they are problems. For my businessman they
were wealth. But all these stars are silent. You – you
alone – will have the stars as no one else has them –'

'What are you trying to say?'

'In one of the stars I shall be living. In one of them I
shall be laughing. And so it will be as if all the stars
were laughing, when you look at the sky at night ...
You – only you – will have stars that can laugh!'

And he laughed again.

'And when your sorrow is comforted (time soothes
all sorrows) you will be content that you have known
me. You will always be my friend. You will want to laugh
with me. And you will sometimes open your window,
so, for that pleasure ... And your friends will be properly
astonished to see you laughing as you look up at the sky!
Then you will say to them, 'Yes, the stars always make
me laugh!' And they will think you are crazy. It will be
a very shabby trick that I shall have played on you ...

And he laughed again.

'It will be as if, in place of the stars, I had given you a great number of little bells that knew how to laugh ...'

And now six years have already gone ... Now my sorrow is comforted a little. That is to say – not entirely. But I know that he did go back to his planet, because I did not find his body at daybreak. It was not such a heavy body ... and at night I love to listen to the stars. It is like five hundred million little bells ...

Antoine de Saint-Exupéry (1900–1944) was a French writer and aviator whose plane disappeared in mysterious circumstances in 1944. This extract is from the last pages of The Little Prince, *his best-known work which, although viewed by some as a simple children's story, is a source of great spiritual comfort to others.*

I Have a Rendevous With Death

POEM

ALAN SEEGER

I have a rendezvous with Death
At some disputed barricade
When Spring comes round with rustling shade
And apple blossoms fill the air.
I have a rendezvous with Death
When Spring brings back blue days and fair.

It may be he shall take my hand
And lead me into his dark land
And close my eyes and quench my breath;
It may be I shall pass him still.
I have a rendezvous with Death
On some scarred slope of battered hill,
When Spring comes round again this year
And the first meadow flowers appear.

God knows 'twere better to be deep
Pillowed in silk and scented down,
Where love throbs out in blissful sleep,
Pulse nigh to pulse, and breath to breath,
Where hushed awakenings are dear ...
But I've a rendezvous with Death
At midnight in some flaming town,
When Spring trips north again this year,
And I to my pledged word am true,
I shall not fail that rendezvous.

137

*Alan Seeger (1888–1916) was an American poet, who died
tragically young in the First World War (1914–1918). Seeger's poems
were published posthumously a year after his death.*

NOVEL

from The Golden Gate

VIKRAM SETH

... Are the dead, too, defiled by sorrow,
Remorse, or anguish? We who love
Clutch at our porous myths to borrow
Belief to ease us, to forgive
Those who by dying have bereft us
Of themselves, of ourselves, and left us
Prey to this spirit-baffling pain.
The countries round our lives maintain
No memoirists and no recorders.
Those who are born are too young, those
Who die are too silent, to disclose
What lies across the occluded borders
Of this bright tract, where we can see
Each other evanescently.

Vikram Seth (b. 1952) is an influential Indian novelist and poet, best known for his novel A Suitable Boy. The Golden Gate *comprises of 690 sonnets and is inspired by Pushkin's* Eugene Onegin.

from Antony and Cleopatra*

WILLIAM SHAKESPEARE

... Noblest of men, woo't die?
Hast thou no care of me? shall I abide
In this dull world, which in thy absence is
No better than a sty? O! see my women,
The crown o' the earth doth melt. My lord!
O! wither'd is the garland of the war,
The soldier's pole is fall'n; young boys and girls
Are level now with men; the odds is gone,
And there is nothing left remarkable
Beneath the visiting moon ...

No more, but e'en a woman, and commanded
By such poor passion as the maid that milks
And does the meanest chares. It were for me
To throw my sceptre at the injurious gods;
To tell them that this world did equal theirs
Till they had stol'n our jewel. All's but naught;
Patience is scottish, and impatience does
Become a dog that's mad; then is it sin
To rush into the secret house of death,
Ere death dare come to us? How do you, women?
What, what! good cheer! Why, how now, Charmian!

139

My noble girls! Ah, women, women, look,
Our lamp is spent, it's out. Good sirs, take heart;–
We'll bury him; and then, what's brave, what's noble,
Let's do it after the high Roman fashion,
And make death proud to take us. Come, away;
This case of that huge spirit now is cold;
Ah! women, women. Come; we have no friend
But resolution, and the briefest end.

*Act IV, Scene xv

William Shakespeare (1564–1616) is one of the most studied playwrights and poets in the English language. He excelled in tragedy, comedy and history. Shakespeare wrote some of the most poignant and moving poetry and prose.

from Cymbeline[*]

WILLIAM SHAKESPEARE

Fear no more the heat o' the sun,
Nor the furious winter's rages;
Thou thy worldly task hast done,
Home art gone, and ta'en thy wages;
Golden lads and girls all must,
As chimney-sweepers, come to dust.

Fear no more the frown o' the great;
Thou art past the tyrant's stroke:
Care no more to clothe and eat;
To thee the reed is as the oak:
The sceptre, learning, physic, must
All follow this, and come to dust.

Fear no more the lightning-flash,
Nor the all-dreaded thunder-stone;
Fear not slander, censure rash;
Thou hast finished joy and moan;
All lovers young, all lovers must
Consign to thee, and come to dust.

No exorciser harm thee!
Nor no witchcraft charm thee!
Ghost unlaid forbear thee!
Nothing ill come near thee!
Quiet consummation have;
And renowned be thy grave.

[*]*Act IV, scene ii*

PLAY

from Romeo and Juliet*

WILLIAM SHAKESPEARE

...When he shall die,
Take him and cut him out in little stars,
And he will make the face of heaven so fine
That all the world will be in love with night,
And pay no worship to the garish sun.

*Act III, scene ii

Juliet about Romeo; President John F. Kennedy
quoted this at the memorial of his brother Robert Kennedy.

142

PLAY

Sonnet 30

WILLIAM SHAKESPEARE

When to the sessions of sweet silent thought
I summon up remembrance of things past,
I sigh the lack of many a thing I sought,
And with old woes new wail my dear times' waste;
Then can I drown an eye, unus'd to flow,
For precious friends hid in death's dateless night,
And weep afresh love's long since cancell'd woe,
And moan the expense of many a vanish'd sight:
Then can I grieve at grievances foregone,
And heavily from woe to woe tell o'er
The sad account of fore-bemoanéd moan,
Which I new pay as if not paid before.
But if the while I think on thee, dear friend,
All losses are restor'd and sorrows end.

Sonnet 60

WILLIAM SHAKESPEARE

Like as the waves make towards the pebbled shore,
So do our minutes hasten to their end,
Each changing place with that which goes before,
In sequent toil all forwards do contend.
Nativity, once in the main of light,
Crawls to maturity, wherewith being crown'd,
Crooked eclipses 'gainst his glory fight,
And Time, that gave, doth now his gift confound.
Time doth transfix the flourish set on youth,
And delves the parallels in beauty's brow;
Feels on the rarities of nature's truth,
And nothing stands but for his scythe to mow.
And yet to times in hope my verse shall stand,
Praising thy worth, despite his cruel hand.

Shakespeare's sonnets were first published in 1609. The 154 sonnets – all but two of which are addressed to a beautiful young man or a treacherous 'dark lady' – deal with eternal subjects such as love and infidelity, memory and mortality, and the destruction wreaked by Time.

Sonnet 71

WILLIAM SHAKESPEARE

No longer mourn for me when I am dead
Than you shall hear the surly sullen bell
Give warning to the world that I am fled
From this vile world, with vilest worms to dwell;
Nay, if you read this line, remember not
The hand that writ it, for I love you so
That I in your sweet thoughts would be forgot,
If thinking on me then you should make you woe.
O if (I say) you look upon this verse,
When I, perhaps, compounded am with clay,
Do not so much as my poor name rehearse,
But let your love even with my life decay;
Lest the wise world should look into your moan,
And mock you with me after I am gone.

Bereavement

POEM

PERCY BYSSHE SHELLEY

How stern are the woes of the desolate mourner
As he bends in still grief o'er the hallowed bier,
As enanguished he turns from the laugh of the scorner,
And drops to perfection's remembrance a tear;
When floods of despair down his pale cheeks are streaming,
When no blissful hope on his bosom is beaming,
Or, if lulled for a while, soon he starts from his dreaming,
And finds torn the soft ties to affection so dear.
Ah, when shall day dawn on the night of the grave,
Or summer succeed to the winter of death?
Rest awhle, hapless victim! and Heaven will save
The spirit that hath faded away with the breath.
Eternity points, in its amaranth bower
Where no clouds of fate o'er the sweet prospect lour,
Unspeakable pleasure, of goodness the dower,
When woe fades away like the mist of the heath.

145

Percy Bysshe Shelley (1792–1822) *was one of the main contributors to the English Romantic Movement whose writing frequently explored themes including love, justice and mortality.*

Music, When Soft Voices Die

PERCY BYSSHE SHELLEY

Music, when soft voices die,
Vibrates in the memory,
Odours, when sweet violets sicken,
Live within the sense they quicken.

Rose leaves, when the rose is dead,
Are heaped for the beloved's bed;
And so thy thoughts, when thou art gone,
Love itself shall slumber on.
When woe fades away like the mist of the heath.

Why Death Is a Blessing

SOCRATES

1 Death is one of two things: either the dead are nothing and have no perception of anything, or death is a relocation of the soul.

2 If death is a complete lack of perception, then death is like a dreamless sleep.

3 A night of dreamless sleep is better than most days and nights in one's life.

4 Thus, if death is a complete lack of perception, it is a blessing. (from 2 and 3)

5 If death is a relocation of the soul, then I (Socrates) will get to spend my time talking with and examining the great figures of history and all others who have died.

6 Talking with and examining the great figures of history and others would be an extraordinary happiness.

7 Thus, if death is a relocation of the soul, it is a blessing. (from 5 and 6)

8 Therefore, death is a blessing. (from 1, 4, and 7)

Socrates (469–399 BC) *was an influential Greek philosopher of Athens. He died by drinking hemlock. This extract is from Socrates'* Apology.

SPIRITUAL

Death Is Not the End

SRI CHINMOY

Death is not the end
Death can never be the end.

Death is the road.
Life is the traveller.
The Soul is the Guide

Our mind thinks of death.
Our heart thinks of life
Our soul thinks of Immortality.

Sri Chinmoy (b. 1931) *was born in East Bengal, India. He is a spiritual writer who has lived and worked in the United States.*

87. In Desperate Hope I Go
from Gitanjali

RABINDRANATH TAGORE

SPIRITUAL

In desperate hope I go and search for her in all
the corners of my room; I find her not.
My house is small and what once has gone from
it can never be regained.
But infinite is thy mansion, my lord, and seeking
her I have come to thy door.
I stand under the golden canopy of thine evening
sky and I lift my eager eyes to thy face.
I have come to the brink of eternity from which
nothing can vanish – no hope, no happiness,
no vision of a face seen through tears.
Oh, dip my emptied life into that ocean, plunge
it into the deepest fullness. Let me for once feel
that lost sweet touch in the allness of the universe.

*Rabindranath Tagore (1861–1941) was a Bengali poet, philosopher
and Nobel Prize winner.* Gitanjali *(or* Song Offerings, *as it is known in English)
was a volume of spiritual verse and was published in 1912.*

POEM

34. Do Not Go My Love
from The Gardener*

RABINDRANATH TAGORE

Do not go, my love, without asking my leave.
I have watched all night, and now my eyes
  are heavy with sleep.
I fear lest I lose you when I'm sleeping.
Do not go, my love, without asking my leave.

I start up and stretch my hands to touch you.
  I ask myself, 'Is it a dream?'
Could I but entangle your feet with my heart
  and hold them fast to my breast!
Do not go, my love, without asking my leave.

150

* *The Gardener* is a volume of poetry, comprising 85 poems in
total, compiled from Rabindranath Tagore's works that were
mainly published between 1896 and 1900.

61. Peace, My Heart
from The Gardener

RABINDRANATH TAGORE

Peace, my heart, let the time for the parting
  be sweet.
Let it not be a death but completeness.
Let love melt into memory and pain into songs.
Let the flight through the sky end in the folding
  of the wings over the nest.
Let the last touch of your hands be gentle like the
  flower of the night.
Stand still, O Beautiful End, for a moment, and
  say your last words in silence.
I bow to you and hold up my lamp to light you
  on your way.

Attitude Toward Death

TECUMSEH, CHIEF OF THE SHAWNEE

Live your life that the fear of death
can never enter your heart.
Trouble no one about his religion.
Respect others in their views
and demand that they respect yours.
Love your life, perfect your life,
beautify all things in your life.
Seek to make your life long
and of service to your people.
Prepare a noble death song for the day
when you go over the great divide.
Always give a word or sign of salute when meeting or
passing a friend, or even a stranger, if in a lonely place.
Show respect to all people, but grovel to none.
When you rise in the morning, give thanks for the
light, for your life, for your strength.
Give thanks for your food and for the joy of living.
If you see no reason to give thanks,
the fault lies in yourself.
Touch not the poisonous firewater that makes wise
ones turn to fools and robs the spirit of its vision.
When your time comes to die, be not like those
whose hearts are filled with fear of death,
so that when their time comes they weep and
pray for a little more time to live their lives over
again in a different way.
Sing your death song, and die like a hero going home.

Tecumseh (1768–1813) was the Chief of the Shawnee, a Native American tribe. He died fighting at the Thames River in Canada in 1813.

In Memoriam
[Ring Out, Wild Bells]

POEM

ALFRED, LORD TENNYSON

Ring out, wild bells, to the wild sky,
The flying cloud, the frosty light:
The year is dying in the night;
Ring out, wild bells, and let him die.

Ring out the old, ring in the new,
Ring, happy bells, across the snow:
The year is going, let him go;
Ring out the false, ring in the true.

Ring out the grief that saps the mind
For those that here we see no more;
Ring out the feud of rich and poor,
Ring in redress to all mankind.

Ring out a slowly dying cause,
And ancient forms of party strife;
Ring in the nobler modes of life,
With sweeter manners, purer laws.

Ring out the want, the care, the sin,
The faithless coldness of the times;
Ring out, ring out my mournful rhymes
But ring the fuller minstrel in.

Ring out false pride in place and blood,
The civic slander and the spite;
Ring in the love of truth and right,
Ring in the common love of good.

Ring out old shapes of foul disease;
Ring out the narrowing lust of gold;
Ring out the thousand wars of old,
Ring in the thousand years of peace.

Ring in the valiant man and free,
The larger heart, the kindlier hand;
Ring out the darkness of the land,
Ring in the Christ that is to be.

Alfred, Lord Tennyson (1809–1892) was perhaps the most popular poet of the Victorian period. He succeeded William Wordsworth as Poet Laureate in 1850. He was described by T.S. Eliot as 'the great master of metric as well as of melancholy.

Tears, Idle Tears

POEM

ALFRED, LORD TENNYSON

Tears, idle tears, I know not what they mean,
Tears from the depth of some divine despair
Rise in the heart, and gather to the eyes,
In looking on the happy autumn-fields,
And thinking of the days that are no more.

Fresh as the first beam glittering on a sail,
That brings our friends up from the underworld,
Sad as the last which reddens over one
That sinks with all we love below the verge;
So sad, so fresh, the days that are no more.

Ah, sad and strange as in dark summer dawns
The earliest pipe of half-awakened birds
To dying ears, when unto dying eyes
The casement slowly grows a glimmering square;
So sad, so strange, the days that are no more.

Dear as remembered kisses after death,
And sweet as those by hopeless fancy feigned
On lips that are for others; deep as love,
Deep as first love, and wild with all regret;
O Death in Life, the days that are no more!

POEM

A Refusal to Mourn the Death, by Fire, of a Child in London

DYLAN THOMAS

Never until the mankind making
Bird beast and flower
Fathering and all humbling darkness
Tells with silence the last light breaking
And the still hour
Is come of the sea tumbling in harness

And I must enter again the round
Zion of the water bead
And the synagogue of the ear of corn
Shall I let pray the shadow of a sound
Or sow my salt seed
In the least valley of sackcloth to mourn

The majesty and burning of the child's death.
I shall not murder
The mankind of her going with a grave truth
Nor blaspheme down the stations of the breath
With any further
Elegy of innocence and youth.

Deep with the first dead lies London's daughter,
Robed in the long friends,
The grains beyond age, the dark veins of her mother,
Secret by the unmourning water
Of the riding Thames.
After the first death, there is no other.

Dylan Thomas (1914–1953) is one of the most famous Welsh poets. He is probably best known for his book Under Milk Wood.

Do Not Go Gentle into That Good Night

POEM

DYLAN THOMAS

Do not go gentle into that good night,
Old age should burn and rave at close of day;
Rage, rage against the dying of the light.
Though wise men at their end know dark is right,
Because their words had forked no lightning they
Do not go gentle into that good night.
Good men, the last wave by, crying how bright
Their frail deeds might have danced in a green bay,
Rage, rage against the dying of the light.
Wild men who caught and sang the sun in flight,
And learn, too late, they grieved it on its way,
Do not go gentle into that good night.
Grave men, near death, who see with blinding sight
Blind eyes could blaze like meteors and be gay,
Rage, rage against the dying of the light.
And you, my father, there on the sad height,
Curse, bless, me now with your fierce tears, I pray.
Do not go gentle into that good night.
Rage, rage against the dying of the light.

POEM

from His Eulogy to His Daughter

MARK TWAIN

Warm summer sun,
  shine brightly here,
Warm Southern wind,
  blow softly here,
Green sod above,
  lie light, lie light,
Good night, dear heart;
  good night, good night.

Mark Twain (1835–1910) was the pseudonym of Samuel Langhorn Clemens. This is taken from his eulogy to his daughter, Olivia Susan Clemens, who died on 18 August 1896, aged 24.

Svetasvatara Upanishad

THE UPANISHADS

...When a man knows God, he is free: his sorrows
have an end, and birth and death are no more.
When in inner union he is beyond the world of
the body, then the third world, the world of the
Spirit, is found, where the power of the All is,
and man has all: for he is one with the ONE.

*The Upanishads are part of the Vedas, the sacred and ancient scriptures
that are the basis of Hinduism. They were composed in Sanskrit between
800 and 400 BC.*

POEM

Time Is

HENRY VAN DYKE

Time is too slow for those who wait,
too swift for those who fear,
too long for those who grieve,
too short for those who rejoice,
but for those who love, time is eternity.

Henry Van Dyke (1852–1933) was an American poet, preacher and critic.

Good Night, Willie Lee, I'll See You in the Morning

ALICE WALKER

POEM

Looking down into my father's
dead face
for the last time
my mother said without
tears, without smiles
but with civility
'Good night, Willie Lee, I'll see you
in the morning.'
And it was then I knew that the healing
of all our wounds
is forgiveness
that permits a promise
of our return
at the end.

Alice Walker (b. 1944) is an African American Pulitzer prize-winning author and poet. This poem was written for her father, Willie Lee, a sharecropper, who helped organise the black voter registrations in Georgia, United States.

POEM

The Old Men Used to Sing

ALICE WALKER

The old men used to sing
And lifted a brother
Carefully
Out the door
I used to think they
Were born
Knowing how to
Gently swing
A casket
They shuffled softly
Eyes dry
More awkward
With the flowers
Than with the widow
After they'd put the
Body in
And stood around waiting
In their
Brown suits.

Each Has His Grief

WALT WHITMAN

On earth are many sights of wo,
And many sounds of agony,
And many a sorrow-wither'd cheek,
And many a pain-dulled eye.

The wretched weep, the poor complain,
And luckless love pines on unknown;
And faintly from the midnight couch
Sounds out the sick-child's moan.

Each has his grief — old age fears death;
The young man's ills are pride, desire,
And heart-sickness; and in his breast
The heat of passion's fire.

And he who runs the race of fame,
Oft feels within a feverish dread,
Lest others snatch the laurel crown
He bears upon his head.

All, all know care; and, at the close,
All lie earth's spreading arms within —
The poor, the black-soul'd, proud, and low,
Virtue, despair, and sin.

O, foolish, then, with pain to shrink
From the sure doom we each must meet.
Is earth so fair — or heaven so dark —
Or life so passing sweet?

No; dread ye not the fearful hour –
The coffin, and the pall's dark gloom,
For there's a calm to throbbing hearts,
And rest, down in the tomb.

Then our long journey will be o'er,
And throwing off earth's load of woes,
The pallid brow, the fainting heart
Will sink in soft repose.

Nor only this: for wise men say
That when we leave our land of care,
We float to a mysterious shore,
Peaceful, and pure, and fair.

So, welcome death! Whene'er the time
That the dread summons must be met,
I'll yield without one pang of fear,
Or sigh, or vain regret.

But like unto a wearied child,
That over field and wood all day
Has ranged and struggled, and at last,
Worn out with toil and play,

Goes up at evening to his home,
And throws him, sleepy, tired, and sore,
Upon his bed, and rests him there,
His pain and trouble o'er.

Walt Whitman (1819–1892) was a groundbreaking American poet.
He is best known for his verse collection Leaves of Grass *which is a*
landmark in the history of American literature.

O Captain! My Captain!*

POEM

WALT WHITMAN

O Captain! my Captain! our fearful trip is done,
The ship has weather'd every rack, the prize we sought is won,
The port is near, the bells I hear, the people all exulting,
While follow eyes the steady keel, the vessel grim and daring;
  But O heart! heart! heart!
    O the bleeding drops of red,
      Where on the deck my Captain lies,
        Fallen cold and dead.

O Captain! my Captain! rise up and hear the bells;
Rise up – for you the flag is flung – for you the bugle trills,
For you bouquets and ribbon'd wreaths – for you the shores
  a-crowding,
For you they call, the swaying mass, their eager faces turning;
  Here Captain! dear father!
    This arm beneath your head!
      It is some dream that on the deck,
        You've fallen cold and dead.

My Captain does not answer, his lips are pale and still,
My father does not feel my arm, he has no pulse nor will,
The ship is anchor'd safe and sound, its voyage closed and done,
From fearful trip, the victor ship, comes in with object won;
  Exult O shores, and ring O bells!
    But I, with mournful tread,
      Walk the deck my Captain lies,
        Fallen cold and dead.

*This poem was written for Abraham Lincoln, President of
the United States of America.

POEM

Youth, Day, Old Age and Night

WALT WHITMAN

Youth, large, lusty, loving-youth full of grace,
  force, fascination,
Do you know that Old Age may come after you
  with equal grace, force, fascination?

Day full-blown and splendid-day of the immense sun,
  action, ambition, laughter,
The Night follows close with millions of suns, and
  sleep and restoring darkness.

Flower of Love

POEM

OSCAR WILDE

Sweet, I blame you not, for mine the fault
was, had I not been made of common clay
I had climbed the higher heights unclimbed
yet, seen the fuller air, the larger day.

From the wildness of my wasted passion I had
struck a better, clearer song,
Lit some lighter light of freer freedom, battled
with some Hydra-headed wrong.

Had my lips been smitten into music by the
kisses that but made them bleed,
You had walked with Bice and the angels on
that verdant and enamelled mead.

I had trod the road which Dante treading saw
the suns of seven circles shine,
Ay! perchance had seen the heavens opening,
as they opened to the Florentine.

And the mighty nations would have crowned
me, who am crownless now and without name,
And some orient dawn had found me kneeling
on the threshold of the House of Fame.

I had sat within that marble circle where the
oldest bard is as the young,
And the pipe is ever dropping honey, and the
lyre's strings are ever strung.

Keats had lifted up his hymeneal curls from out
the poppy-seeded wine,
With ambrosial mouth had kissed my forehead,
clasped the hand of noble love in mine.

And at springtide, when the apple-blossoms
brush the burnished bosom of the dove,
Two young lovers lying in an orchard would
have read the story of our love;

Would have read the legend of my passion,
known the bitter secret of my heart,
Kissed as we have kissed, but never parted as
we two are fated now to part.

For the crimson flower of our life is eaten by
the cankerworm of truth,
And no hand can gather up the fallen withered
petals of the rose of youth.

Yet I am not sorry that I loved you – ah!
what else had I a boy to do, –
For the hungry teeth of time devour, and the
silent-footed years pursue.

Rudderless, we drift athwart a tempest, and
when once the storm of youth is past,
Without lyre, without lute or chorus, Death
the silent pilot comes at last.

And within the grave there is no pleasure,
for the blindworm battens on the root,
And Desire shudders into ashes, and the tree
of Passion bears no fruit.

Ah! what else had I to do but love you?
God's own mother was less dear to me,
And less dear the Cytheraean rising like an
argent lily from the sea.

I have made my choice, have lived my
poems, and, though youth is gone in wasted days,
I have found the lover's crown of myrtle better
than the poet's crown of bays.

*Oscar Wilde (1855–1900) was an Irish poet, dramatist,
wit and acclaimed member of 19th-century literary society.*

Requiescat

OSCAR WILDE

TREAD lightly, she is near
Under the snow,
Speak gently, she can hear
The daisies grow.

All her bright golden hair
Tarnished with rust,
She that was young and fair
Fallen to dust.

Lily-like, white as snow,
She hardly knew
She was a woman, so
Sweetly she grew.

Coffin-board, heavy stone,
Lie on her breast,
I vex my heart alone,
She is at rest.

Peace, peace, she cannot hear
Lyre or sonnet,
All my life's buried here,
Heap earth upon it.

from Her Eulogy to Rosa Parks[*]

OPRAH WINFREY

... And in that moment when you resolved to stay in that seat, you reclaimed your humanity and you gave us all back a piece of our own. I thank you for that. I thank you for acting without concern. I often thought about what that took ... You acted without concern for yourself and made life better for us all. We shall not be moved. I marvel at your will. I celebrate your strength to this day. And I am forever grateful ... for your courage, your conviction. I owe you to succeed. I will not be moved.

[*] Rosa Parks (1913–2005) was a leading black Civil Rights activist, who refused to give up her seat to a white person on a bus, thereby leading others to passively resist the discriminatory treatment that African Americans received in the United States.

Oprah Winfrey (b. 1954) is one of the most influential African American women in the world. A leading media commentator, Winfrey has dedicated her life to improving civil and human rights for people around the world. Parks was an inspiration for her and she made this speech at her memorial on 31 October 2005.

POEM

Daffodils

WILLIAM WORDSWORTH

I WANDER'D lonely as a cloud
That floats on high o'er vales and hills,
When all at once I saw a crowd,
A host, of golden daffodils;
Beside the lake, beneath the trees,
Fluttering and dancing in the breeze.

Continuous as the stars that shine
And twinkle on the Milky Way,
They stretch'd in never-ending line
Along the margin of a bay:
Ten thousand saw I at a glance,
Tossing their heads in sprightly dance.

The waves beside them danced; but they
Out-did the sparkling waves in glee:
A poet could not but be gay,
In such a jocund company:
I gazed – and gazed – but little thought
What wealth the show to me had brought:

For oft, when on my couch I lie
In vacant or in pensive mood,
They flash upon that inward eye
Which is the bliss of solitude;
And then my heart with pleasure fills,
And dances with the daffodils.

William Wordsworth (1770–1850) *helped launch the English Romantic Movement with the publication of* Lyrical Ballads *(1798) in collaboration with Samuel Taylor Coleridge. Wordsworth wrote poetry that explored nature, which was viewed by the Romantics as divine.*

Farewell, Sweet Dust

POEM

ELINOR WYLIE

Now I have lost you, I must scatter
All of you on the air henceforth;
Not that to me it can ever matter
But it's only fair to the rest of the earth.

Now especially, when it is winter
And the sun's not half as bright as it was,
Who wouldn't be glad to find a splinter
That once was you, in the frozen grass?

Snowflakes, too, will be softer feathered,
Clouds, perhaps, will be whiter plumed;
Rain, whose brilliance you caught and gathered,
Purer silver have resumed.

Farewell, sweet dust; I never was a miser:
Once, for a minute, I made you mine:
Now you are gone, I am none the wiser
But the leaves of the willow are as bright as wine.

Elinor Wylie (1885–1928) was an American poet and novelist.
Her poetry is influenced by the poetry of 16th and 17th century England.

POEM

An Irish Airman* Foresees His Death

W.B. YEATS

I know that I shall meet my fate
Somewhere among the clouds above;
Those that I fight I do not hate,
Those that I guard I do not love;
My country is Kiltartan Cross,
My countrymen Kiltartan's poor,
No likely end could bring them loss
Or leave them happier than before.

Nor law, nor duty bade me fight,
Nor public men, nor cheering crowds,
A lonely impulse of delight
Drove to this tumult in the clouds;
I balanced all, brought all to mind,
The years to come seemed waste of breath,
A waste of breath the years behind
In balance with this life, this death.

174

*This was written about Major Robert Gregory (1881–1918),
the only child of W.B. Yeats's great friend Lady Augusta Gregory.

*W.B. Yeats (1865–1939) was an influential Irish poet. He won
the Nobel Prize for literature. His poetry often draws upon Irish myth
and legend and often deals with subjects such as war, struggle and death.*

The Sorrow of Love*

W.B. YEATS

POEM

The quarrel of the sparrows in the eaves,
The full round moon and the star-laden sky,
And the loud song of the ever-singing leaves,
Had hid away earth's old and weary cry.

And then you came with those red mournful lips,
And with you came the whole of the world's tears,
And all the sorrows of her labouring ships,
And all the burden of her myriad years.

And now the sparrows warring in the eaves,
The curd-pale moon, the white stars in the sky,
And the loud chaunting of the unquiet leaves
Are shaken with earth's old and weary cry.

*This was written in 1891, two years after Yeats met and
fell in love with Maud Gonne.

POEM

Upon a Dying Lady

W.B. YEATS

I
Her Courtesy

WITH the old kindness, the old distinguished grace,
She lies, her lovely piteous head amid dull red hair
propped upon pillows, rouge on the pallor of her face.
She would not have us sad because she is lying there,
And when she meets our gaze her eyes are laughter-lit,
Her speech a wicked tale that we may vie with her,
Matching our broken-hearted wit against her wit,
Thinking of saints and of petronius Arbiter.

II
Curtain Artist bring her Dolls and Drawings

Bring where our Beauty lies
A new modelled doll, or drawing,
With a friend's or an enemy's
Features, or maybe showing
Her features when a tress
Of dull red hair was flowing
Over some silken dress
Cut in the Turkish fashion,
Or, it may be, like a boy's.
We have given the world our passion,
We have naught for death but toys.

III
She turns the Dolls' Faces to the Wall

Because to-day is some religious festival
They had a priest say Mass, and even the Japanese,
Heel up and weight on toe, must face the wall
– Pedant in passion, learned in old courtesies,
Vehement and witty she had seemed –; the Venetian lady
Who had seemed to glide to some intrigue in her red shoes,
Her domino, her panniered skirt copied from Longhi;
The meditative critic; all are on their toes,
Even our Beauty with her Turkish trousers on.
Because the priest must have like every dog his day
Or keep us all awake with baying at the moon,
We and our dolls being but the world were best away.

IV
The End of Day

She is playing like a child
And penance is the play,
Fantastical and wild
Because the end of day
Shows her that some one soon
Will come from the house, and say –
Though play is but half done –
'Come in and leave the play.'

V
Her Race

She has not grown uncivil
As narrow natures would
And called the pleasures evil
Happier days thought good;
She knows herself a woman,
No red and white of a face,
Or rank, raised from a common
Unreckonable race;
And how should her heart fail her
Or sickness break her will
With her dead brother's valour
For an example still?

VI
Her Courage

When her soul flies to the predestined dancing-place
(I have no speech but symbol, the pagan speech I made
Amid the dreams of youth) let her come face to face,
Amid that first astonishment, with Grania's shade,
All but the terrors of the woodland flight forgot
That made her Diatmuid dear, and some old cardinal
Pacing with half-closed eyelids in a sunny spot
Who had murmured of Giorgione at his latest breath –
Aye, and Achilles, Timor, Babar, Barhaim, all
Who have lived in joy and laughed into the face of Death.

VII
Her Friends bring her a Christmas Tree

Pardon, great enemy,
Without an angry thought
We've carried in our tree,
And here and there have bought
Till all the boughs are gay,
And she may look from the bed
On pretty things that may
Please a fantastic head.
Give her a little grace,
What if a laughing eye
Have looked into your face?
It is about to die.

Reflections on Grief, Life & Death

'Death was afraid of him because he had the heart of a lion.'
–Arabian proverb

'Death is the sound of distant thunder at a picnic.'
– W.H. Auden (1907–1973), poet

'... Perhaps the whole root of our trouble, the human trouble, is that we will sacrifice all the beauty of our lives, will imprison ourselves in totems, taboos, crosses, blood sacrifices, steeples, mosques, races, armies, flags, nations, in order to deny the fact of death, which is the only fact we have.'
– James Baldwin (1924–1987),
writer and Civil Rights activist

'Any relic of the dead is precious, if they were valued living.'
– Emily Bronte (1818–1848),
novelist and poet

'I shall not die of a cold. I shall die of having lived.'
– Willa Cather (1873–1947), writer

'Life is a dream walking, death is a going home.'
– Chinese Proverb

*'That last day does not bring extinction to us,
but change of place.'*
– Marcus Tulius Cicero (106–43 BC),
writer, politician and orator

*'As a well-spent day brings happy sleep, so a life
well spent brings happy death.'*
– Leonardo da Vinci (1452–1519), painter,
sculptor and architect

*'Death is a Dialogue between the Spirit
and the Dust.'*
– Emily Dickinson (1830–1886), poet.

'Dying is a wild night and a new road.'
– Emily Dickinson

'To die is landing on some distant shore.'
– John Dryden (1631–1700), poet,
dramatist and critic

*'Our death is not an end if we can live on in
our children and the younger generation.
For they are us, our bodies are only
wilted leaves on the tree of life.'*
– Albert Einstein (1879–1955),
scientist

*'Death destroys a man, but the idea
of death saves him.'*
– E.M. Forster (1879–1970),
novelist and essayist '

Death is a commingling of eternity with time; in the death of a good man, eternity is seen looking through time.'
– Johann Wolfgang von Goethe (1749–1832), poet, novelist and dramatist

'Say not in grief he is no more but live in thankfulness that he was.'
– Hebrew proverb

'There's something about death that is comforting. The thought that you could die tomorrow frees you to appreciate life now.'
– Angelina Jolie (b. 1975), actor

'If we really think that home is elsewhere and that this life is a "wandering to find home," why should we not look forward to the arrival?'
– C.S. Lewis (1898–1963), author and scholar

'Every man must do two things alone; he must do his own believing and his own dying.'
– Martin Luther (1483–1546), priest and scholar

'The world is the mirror of myself dying.'
– Henry Miller (1891–1980), author

'Death makes angels of us all and gives us wings where we had shoulders smooth as raven's claws.'
– Jim Morrison (1943–1971), singer

'... To die proudly when it is no longer possible to live proudly. Death of one's own free choice, death at the proper time, with a clear head and with joyfulness, consummated in the midst of children and witnesses: so that an actual leave-taking is possible while he who is leaving is still there.'
– Friedrich Nietzsche (1844–1900), philosopher, scholar and writer

'Every man goes down to his death bearing in his hands only that which he has given away.'
– Persian proverb

'Know one knows whether death, which people fear to be the greatest evil, may not be the greatest good.'
– Plato (427– 347 BC), philosopher

'People do not die for us immediately, but remain bathed in a sort of aura of life which bears no relation to true immortality but through which they continue to occupy our thoughts in the same way as when they were alive. It is as though they were travelling abroad.'
– Marcel Proust (1871–1922), writer

'Good men must die, but death cannot kill their names.'
– Proverb

'After all, to the well-organised mind, death is but the next great adventure.'
– J.K. Rowling (b. 1965), writer

'When the body sinks into death, the essence of man is revealed. Man is a knot, a web, a mesh into which relationships are tied. Only those relationships matter. The body is an old crock that nobody will miss. I have never known a man to think of himself when dying. Never.'
– Antoine de Saint-Exupéry (1900–1944),
aviator and writer

'One approaches the journey's end. But the end is a goal, not a catastrophe.'
– George Sand (1804–1876),
Romantic writer

'All that live must die, passing through nature to eternity.'
– William Shakespeare (1564–1616),
poet and playwright

'Death may be the greatest of all human blessings.'
– Socrates (469–399 BC),
philosopher of Athens

'The hour of departure has arrived and we go our ways; I to die, and you to live. Which is better? Only God knows.'
– Socrates

'It is perfectly certain that the soul is immortal and imperishable, and our souls will actually exist in another world.'
– Socrates

*'Death is an endless night so awful to contemplate
that it can make us love life and value it with
such passion that it may be the ultimate cause
of all joy and all art.'*
– Paul Theroux (b. 1941), novelist
and travel writer

*'Live your life, do your work,
then take your hat.'*
– Henry David Thoreau (1817–1862),
naturalist, poet and philosopher

*'Nothing can happen more
beautiful than death.'*
– Walt Whitman (1819–1892), poet

*'Once can survive everything nowadays,
except death.'*
– Oscar Wilde (1854–1900),
poet and dramatist

*'Death is nature's way of saying
your table's ready.'*
– Robin Williams (b. 1951),
actor and comedian

*'Against you I will fling myself, unvanquished
and unyielding, O Death!'*
– Virginia Woolf (1882–1941),
novelist and essayist

Acknowledgements

I would like to thank the very many great writers whose work appears in this book and whose words have sustained me in times of grief and sorrow. I would also like to thank my publisher, Aruna Vasudevan, and editor, Julia Shone, at New Holland, for both commissioning this work and also for putting in the time and dedication it takes to put any book, particularly a collection, together.

Every effort has been made to contact copyright holders, but should there be any omissions, New Holland Publishers would be pleased to insert the appropriate acknowledgement in any subsequent printing of this publication.

'Memorial Day for the War Dead' from *Amen* by Yehuda Amichai. Copyright © 1977 by Yehuda Amichai. Reprinted by permission of HarperCollins Publishers. From *Three Greek Plays* Prometheus Bound, Agamemnon, and The Trojan Women, translated by Edith Hamilton. Copyright 1937 by W.W. Norton and Company, Inc., renewed © 1965 by Doris Fielding Reid. Used by permission of W.W. Norton & Company, Inc. 'Refusal' from *Complete Collected Poems of Maya Angelou* by Maya Angelou. Copyright © 1994 by Maya Angelou. Used by permission of Random House, Inc. In the UK and British Commonwealth: reprinted by permission of Virago, an imprint of Little, Brown Book Group. 'I Thought I'd Write My Own Obituary Instead' from *Book of Matches* by Simon Armitage. Reprinted by permission of Faber and Faber Ltd. 'Twelve Songs IX' and 'The Unknown Citizen' from *Collected Poems* by W.H. Auden. Reprinted by permission of Faber and Faber Ltd. In the US: 'The Unknown Citizen', copyright 1940 and renewed 1968 by W.H. Auden, 'Funeral Blues', copyright 1940 and renewed 1968 by W.H. Auden, from *Collected Poems* by W.H. Auden. Used by permission of Random House, Inc. Excerpt from *The Gift of Peace: Personal Reflections by Joseph Cardinal Bernardin* (Loyola Press,

1997). Reprinted with permission of Loyola Press. Extract from *Letters And Papers From Prison* by Dietrich Bonhoeffer, reproduced by permission of SCM-Canterbury Press Ltd. In the US: reprinted with the permission of Scribner, a Division of Simon and Schuster, Inc., from *Letters And Papers From Prison*, Revised, Enlarged Ed. by Dietrich Bonhoeffer. (Translated from the German by R. H. Fuller, Frank Clark, et al) Copyright © 1953, 1967, 1971 by SCM Press Ltd. All rights reserved. 'My Death' Music and Original French lyrics by Jacques Brel – English lyrics by Eric Blau and Mort Shuman © 1967 Pouchenel Editions Musicales. Reproduced by kind permission of Carlin Music Corp., London, NW1 8BD, England. 'I'm Here for a Short Visit Only' from *Noel Coward Collected Verse* by Noel Coward. Reprinted by permission of Methuen Drama, an imprint of A&C Black Publishers. 'dying is fine)but Death' is reprinted from *Complete Poems 1904-1962* by E.E. Cummings, edited by George J. Firmage, by permission of W.W. Norton & Company, Copyright © 1991 by the Trustees for the E.E. Cummings Trust and George James Firmage. 'Because I Could Not Stop For Death', 'Not In Vain', 'I Measure Every Grief I Meet' and 'Tie the Strings to My Life, My Lord' by Emily Dickinson, reprinted by permission of the publishers and the Trustees of Amherst College from *The Poems Of Emily Dickinson*, Thomas H. Johnson, ed., Cambridge, Mass.: The Belknap Press of Harvard University Press, Copyright © 1951, 1955, 1979, 1983 by the President and Fellows of Harvard College. 'Nothing Gold Can Stay', 'The Road Not Taken' and 'Out, Out' from *The Poetry Of Robert Frost* edited by Edward Connery Lathem, published by Jonathan Cape. Reprinted by permission of The Random House Group Ltd. Extract from 'On Joy and Sorrow' from *The Prophet* by Kahlil Gibran, copyright 1923 by Kahlil Gibran and renewed 1951 by Administrators C.T.A. of Kahlil Gibran Estate and Mary G. Gibran. Used by permission of Alfred A. Knopf, a division of Random House, Inc. 'If I Should Go Before The Rest Of You' by Joyce Grenfell © Joyce Grenfell Memorial Trust 1980. Reproduced by permission of Sheil Land Associates Ltd. Patrick Kavanagh's 'Memory of My Father' is reprinted from *Collected Poems*, edited by Antoinette Quinn (Allen Lane, 2004), by kind permission of the Trustees of the Estate of the late Katherine B. Kavanagh, through the Jonathan Williams Literary Agency. Li-Young Lee, 'From Blossoms' from *Rose*. Copyright © 1986 by Li-Young Lee. Reprinted with the permission of BOA Editions, Ltd., www.boaeditions.org. *A Grief Observed* by C.S. Lewis copyright © C.S. Lewis Pte. Ltd. 1961. Extract reprinted by permission. 'Of You' from *The Poems Of Norman MacCaig* by Norman MacCaig is reproduced by permission of Polygon, an imprint of Birlinn Ltd www.birlinn.co.uk 'Meeting Point' from *Collected Poems* by Louis Macniece. Published by Faber and Faber Ltd. Extract from *The House At Pooh Corner* by A.A. Milne. Copyright © The Trustees of the Pooh Properties, reproduced with permission of Curtis Brown Group, Ltd. London. 'A Song of Despair' from *Twenty Love Poems and a Song Of Despair* by Pablo Neruda, translated by W. S. Merwin, published by Jonathan Cape. Reprinted by permission of The Random House Group Ltd. In the United States: used by permission of Viking Penguin, a division of Penguin Group (USA) Inc. Sonnet LXXXIX from *100 Love Sonnets: Cien Sonetos De Amor* by Pablo Neruda, translated by Stephen Tapscott, copyright © Pablo Neruda 1959 and Fundacion Pablo Neruda, Copyright © 1986 by the University of Texas Press. By permission of the University of Texas Press. 'The Moon and the Yew Tree' from *Collected Poems* by Sylvia Plath. Copyright © The Estate of Sylvia Plath. Reprinted by permission of Faber and Faber Ltd. Extract from *The Gitanjali:87*, The Gardener:34 and The Gardener:61 by Rabindranath Tagore, reprinted by permission of the Sahitya Akademi. 'An Irish Airman Foresees His Death', 'The Sorrow of Love' and 'Upon a Dying Lady' by W.B. Yeats reproduced by permission of A.P. Watt Ltd on behalf of Grainne Yeats. Scripture quotations taken from the Holy Bible, New International Version. Copyright © 1973, 1978, 1984 by International Bible Society. Used by permission of Hodder & Stoughton Publishers, A member of the Hachette Livre UK Group. All rights reserved.

Index of First Lines